Enlightened

Getting rich with Ancient Wisdom And AI
A Guide to Financial Independence

Bringing generations together and growing abundance

Table of Contents

Module 1:
Introduction to Financial Independence

Chapter 1: Exploring Financial Freedom

Chapter 2: The Universal Law of Attraction and AI

Chapter 3: Aligning Values and Goals

Chapter 4: Practical Ways to Create Wealth for Families

Chapter 5: The Ancient Law of Giving and Receiving

Chapter 6: Ancient Principles of Mindfulness and Abundance

Chapter 7: AI-Driven Insights into Cause and Effect

Chapter 8: Practical Business Ideas: Ancient Wisdom and AI-Enhanced Concepts

Module 2:
Foundations of Abundance

Chapter 9: Budgeting with Ancient Wisdom and AI

Chapter 10: Ethical Investing: Balancing Ancient Virtues and AI

Chapter 11: Wealth Accumulation Strategies through Ages and Algorithms

Chapter 12: Practical Money-Making Ventures for Families

Module 3:
Financial Health and Well-being

Module 4:
The Journey to Wealth Creation

Module 5:
Expanding Horizons: Global Perspectives on Wealth

Module 6:
Future of finance and AI

Module 7:
Financial Independence and Personal Growth

Module 8:

Legacy of Enlightenment

Empowering Future Generations with Financial Wisdom.

The Need for Enlightened Wealth.

Wealth growth, wealth transfer, and, most importantly, the desire to do more are all part of the story of human history. But as society has changed, our idea of what "wealth" really means has changed in a big way. People are becoming more aware of the idea of "enlightened wealth." It's no longer just about having a lot of money. But what is enlightened wealth, and why is it so important in the modern world, especially when compared to old knowledge and AI?

1. Understanding Enlightened Wealth

Enlightened wealth is more than just having a lot of money. It shows that you have a good mix of financial security, intellectual growth, spiritual depth, and a desire to help other people. It says that financial freedom is important, but it's only one part of being happy and healthy generally.

2. Historical Perspective on Wealth

In the past, many ancient civilizations thought that wealth wasn't just having gold or land, but also having a lot of information, wisdom, and good character. In ancient India, for example, people thought that true success was a mix of "Artha" (material wealth) and "Dharma" (living the right way). Socrates and other old Greek philosophers believed in the wealth of the soul and stressed the importance of self- knowledge and virtue.

3. The Limitations of Material Wealth.

Material wealth can give you comfort, security, and chances, but it can only do so much. It can't buy happiness, a sense of purpose, or peace of mind. Many people find themselves on a never-ending treadmill of getting more things when they depend too much on their material wealth. This can cause stress, anxiety, and a feeling of nothingness.

4. AI and the Modern Perception of Wealth.

With the rise of AI and data-driven decision making, we now have tools that can help us predict, improve, and optimize our financial choices. But as AI makes it easier to get rich, it also shows how pointless it is to try to get rich just for the sake of getting rich. People are becoming more aware that technology should serve more than just their cash.

5. The Role of Enlightened Wealth in Society.

When people try to get informed wealth, it sends waves through society. They are more likely to spend in important causes, support ethical and environmentally friendly practices, and help the community grow. Here, ancient wisdom, which focuses on community and well-being as a whole, matches up with the abilities of AI, which can find and support these larger goals for society.

6. Achieving Personal Fulfillment.

Enlightened wealth gives you a greater sense of satisfaction on a personal level. People find that their journey to financial freedom is also a journey of personal growth, self-awareness, and satisfaction when they understand and align with their core values and purpose.

7. How ancient wisdom, AI, and enlightened wealth work together

When old knowledge and AI come together, it creates a unique chance. AI gives us the tools to make this idea a reality in the modern world. Ancient principles give us a moral compass that points us toward holistic prosperity. By using the best parts of both, people can start down a road to enlightened wealth that is good for them and for society as a whole.

Conclusion

There has never been a greater need for wise wealth. In a world where people have more and more things, people are looking for purpose, connection, and greater meaning. By embracing the principles of enlightened wealth, which are based on the wisdom of the ancients and the capabilities of modern AI, we can plot a path toward a more holistic, fulfilling, and sustainable future.

The Ancient and AI Roadmap to Enlightened Wealth

"The Ancient and AI Roadmap to Enlightened Wealth" isn't just another financial guide; it's a fascinating journey that spans eras and innovations, rethinking wealth in vivid, resonant colors. By picking this book, you're choosing to think about more than just money. You're choosing to connect wealth with a sense of meaning and real well-being. Let it take you back to times when wealth wasn't just about things you could touch but also about ideas that last. As you move forward, find out how modern AI can boost and improve these strategies, making it easier for you to get to a future that is rich not only in assets but also in values and goals. This book is a call to live a fuller, more harmonious life, where your riches are in tune with the deepest desires of your soul. It's a confident step through the uncertain financial world of today, a dance between trusted ancient knowledge and the precise, cutting-edge insights of AI. And as the world struggles with moral and environmental problems, this book shines like a lighthouse, showing how to get rich in a way that cares about both individual needs and the future of the whole world. It's written for everyone, from a seasoned business owner to a new investor. It tells interesting stories and gives practical advice to make financial dreams come true. It's more than just lines on paper; it's a powerful pull toward a new way of thinking about money. Every statement and every piece of information is a step toward enlightened wealth. So, are you ready to start the most enlightening trip you'll ever take with your money? This book is more than just something to read—it's an adventure into the heart of real wealth. Jump in and find out.

The Preface

As the sun goes down, it makes long shadows that connect modern skyscrapers to old temples, making a bridge between two worlds that seem very different. The whole point of "The Ancient and AI Roadmap to Enlightened Wealth" is to show how the old and the new can live together.

People have always struggled with the idea of wealth—how to get it, keep it, and figure out what it really means. The wisdom of our ancestors, which comes from the heartbeats of ancient societies, tells us a lot about what it means to be successful. These aren't just stories about treasure troves or golden ages; they also have deep lessons about how to balance material goals with the soul's greater desires.

Artificial intelligence is a wonder of our time that promises to change everything about our lives, including how we think about money. AI isn't just about algorithms and data; it's also about improving our skills and strategies, and in this book, it's about making sure that our financial goals are in line with social and whole-person concerns.

This book doesn't just mix old and new ideas; it's a symphony. A balance between knowledge from the past and ideas about the future. It's a call to change the way you think about wealth, to look beyond your bank statements and into a deeper world of prosperity that balances material gain with spiritual wealth.

As you read these pages, you'll start on a journey that will change you. From the busy markets of ancient Silk Road towns to the digital financial hubs powered by quantum computing, you'll find strategies, stories, and lessons that are both old and new.

I want you to think of this not just as a book but also as a compass—a map that not only helps you with your finances but also shows you what real wealth is. Let's go on a trip together to make a plan for enlightened wealth, which is money that makes our lives and souls better as well as our pockets.

Welcome to the journey of your life Join in.

Sincerely, Anant

Module 1:
Introduction to Financial Independence

Chapter 1: Exploring Financial Freedom

Chapter 2: The Universal Law of Attraction and AI

Chapter 3: Aligning Values and Goals

Chapter 4: Practical Ways to Create Wealth for Families

Chapter 5: The Ancient Law of Giving and Receiving

Chapter 6: Ancient Principles of Mindfulness and Abundance

Chapter 7: AI-Driven Insights into Cause and Effect

Chapter 8: Practical Business Ideas: Ancient Wisdom and AI-Enhanced Concepts

Chapter 1: Exploring Financial Freedom

Defining Financial Independence

In the soft glow of a setting sun or the first chirps of birds at dawn, nature shows how free it is by being itself. Just like these things don't need permission to happen, financial independence is about having the same freedom with our money. But what does it really mean to have your own money?

At first look, it might seem like having enough money to never have to work again is the same thing as being financially independent. Even though this is a part of it, there is much more to it than this. It's not just about getting rich, but also about overseeing it. It's about being able to make decisions that aren't limited by money, being able to live life on your own terms, and being able to follow your interests without worrying about bills or debts.

Imagine a life where you don't have to keep an eye on the time, count down the days until your next paycheck, or worry about the next unexpected cost. Being financially independent gives you the freedom to breathe, travel, dream, and take risks. It's the link between personal goals and the realities of everyday life, making a flow of opportunities possible.

In the past, people thought that wealth meant having a lot of land, having a lot of crops, or having cash treasures. But as time went on and communities changed, so did people's ideas about what wealth was. Today, when digital currencies and global interests are common, being financially independent means being strong, flexible, and in charge of your own life. It's about building a life where money supports your goals instead of dictating them.

But there is no secret recipe or one-size-fits-all plan for getting to this state. It's a unique journey with its own set of problems and wins. The journey is a worship, not an effort or a race. A quest to find that holy spot where your financial situation and your deepest values and goals match up As we go deeper into this chapter and the ones that come after it, you'll find out that financial freedom is made up of many different parts. You'll find out how ancient knowledge and modern tactics come together to help you get to this coveted place. Whether you're just starting out on your financial journey or trying to get back on track, this chapter is meant to educate, excite, and guide you toward a life in which money is not a master but a tool—a tool that leads to real freedom.

Join me on this enlightening journey as we explore the landscapes of financial freedom and learn about the deep joys of real financial independence.

Ancient Wisdom's Perspective on Financial Freedom

For thousands of years, the winds that blow through the ancient woods have told stories of wealth and abundance. There is a deep understanding of wealth and financial freedom that can be found in the shadow of old pyramids, in the middle of busy ancient markets, and in the wise words of thinkers from long ago.

To understand financial freedom through the lens of ancient wisdom, we must first go back in time to places where trust, honor, and knowledge were used as money instead of gold or silver.

Artha was one of the four main goals of life, according to the old Indian Vedic traditions. It means wealth, but what it really means is the tools and means one needs to live a full, balanced life. Wealth wasn't a goal in and of itself. Instead, it was a tool that helped people reach their bigger goals of doing the right thing, having fun, and, in the end, spiritual freedom.

Confucian and Daoist teachings had a big impact on ancient Chinese thought, which saw wealth as being in harmony with nature and the flow of life. Wealth was seen as a sign of the natural abundance of the universe, but it came with a caveat: it should be sought in an upright manner that doesn't hurt one's virtues.

Philosophers like Aristotle, who lived in the busy marketplaces of ancient Greece, thought that the middle road, or the "Golden Mean," was the way to go. Wealth was important, but too much of it was looked upon. Financial independence didn't mean having a lot of money, but rather having enough to live a good life and take care of both the mind and society.

Traditional African groups like the Maasai valued cattle not just for trade, but also as a sign of wealth and social status. But their knowledge also focused on keeping the community in balance and making sure that making money didn't use up resources or cause problems.

All of these old ideas have in common the idea that financial freedom isn't just about getting rich for yourself. Balance is the key. It's a place where one's material and spiritual needs and wants are in balance. In many traditions, wealth is still a sign of how well someone is in tune with the world, society, and themselves.

Compare this to the world we live in now, and you'll see some surprising similarities. Even though we have complicated financial tools, digital currencies, and global markets now, the basic idea is still the same. Financial freedom isn't just about getting rich; it's about getting to a point where our wealth matches up with what we value inside.

Remember this basic advice as we move through the next chapters and learn more about current strategies and techniques that use AI. Even though these old cultures are different and unique, they all show us the way to financial freedom that is not just rich but also meaningful and deep. In their teachings, we can find a way to get rich that is good for the soul, helps the community, and fits in with the rest of the world.

Synergy of Ancient Principles and AI-Enhanced Strategies

In the complex pattern of time, there are two threads that stand out: the golden thread of ancient knowledge and the shimmering thread of new technology. Even though they seem very different, when these threads are woven together, they make a pattern with a lot of promise. When it comes to financial freedom, the combination of age-old principles and AI-enhanced methods can give you a new way of looking at things.

People have been looking for patterns since the beginning of society. They look for them in the sky, in the way the seasons change, and in the way rivers flow. We've always been interested in trying to figure out how the world works and use its resources. Ancient people, from the Indus Valley to the Mayans, used complex systems and ideas to figure out what these patterns meant and make choices that would lead to peace and prosperity.

This search for patterns in the past is similar to how AI works at its core in many ways. AI is, at its core, a modern tool for finding patterns in big data, economic trends, and customer behavior. It's like the Oracle of Babylon for the digital age, making predictions based on complicated formulas.

Think about what could happen when these two strong forces work together.

By combining the big-picture insights of ancient knowledge with the accuracy of AI analytics, we can come up with financial strategies that are both solid and new. Ancient principles remind us of how important balance, ethics, and sustainability are, but AI gives us practical, data-driven ways to reach these goals in today's complicated financial world.

Think about the old rule of diversity. Ancient sellers knew right away that putting all their eggs in one basket was risky. They changed how they traded, what they traded, and who they worked with. With the help of AI, this concept is now carried out with the accuracy of surgery. Algorithms look at global market trends, international risks, and even environmental factors. This helps investors diversify their portfolios in real time, maximizing returns while minimizing risks.

Or think about the age-old virtues of being patient and having a long-term view. Ancient societies that farmed knew how important it was to plant seeds carefully, care for them, and wait calmly for the harvest. In the world of investing, AI tools can help with this by sorting through short-term market noise to find long-term growth chances. This makes sure that we stay patient and don't make decisions on the spot.

But AI isn't just about improving old ways of doing things. It's also important to make sure that as we use AI's power, we don't lose sight of the ethical foundations and whole person concerns that ancient wisdom promotes. As AI opens up new areas in fintech, like algorithmic trading and robo-advisors, it's important to base these new ideas on values that have been around for a long time. This makes sure that the chase of wealth doesn't come at the expense of doing good for society or finding personal happiness.

In this chapter, we'll go into more detail about some of the places where old knowledge and AI meet, giving readers a road map that's both traditional and revolutionary. When the old and the new, the spiritual and the scientific, work together, it can pave the way for a financially successful journey that is also meaningful and enlightening. Join us as we start this exciting journey and plot a path to a future where technology and ritual dance together in perfect harmony

Chapter 2: The Universal Law of Attraction and AI

How the Ancient Law of Attraction Works

At its core, the Universal Law of Attraction is an old idea that has been passed down through different countries, beliefs, and traditions. This law is often summed up by the saying, "Like attracts like." It says that the energy we give off, whether it's positive or negative, works like a magnet, drawing similar experiences, situations, and even people into our lives.

Before we get into the details, let's take a trip back to the old world, where these ideas first began to grow.

In India's holy Vedic texts, there is a word called "Rishi," which means "to see" or "seer." It shows that our thoughts, feelings, and inner visions have the power to change the world around us. In the same way, ancient Buddhist texts talk about the law of karma, which says that our intentions and actions (which often come from our thoughts) spread out into the world and come back to us in the same way.

In Ancient Greece, the famous philosopher Heraclitus said, "Character is destiny." This shows that our internal state, our character, and the way we think will always shape our external world and our fate.

In more recent times, books like 'The Secret' brought the Law of Attraction back into the spotlight. But it's important to remember that this isn't a "new age" idea. It's a timeless principle that wise people, thinkers, and visionaries have known, honored, and used throughout history.

But what does all this mean in real life? Imagine the world as a huge, complex mirror. It shows us the energies, thoughts, and feelings we send out into the world. When we think about having enough, doing well, and being happy, we tend to attract experiences and chances that match these energies. On the other hand, if we stay stuck in a vortex of negativity, fear, or lack, the world reflects these back to us as well.

Now, you might be wondering how the cold, logical world of Artificial Intelligence relates to this old, mysterious idea.

As we go through this chapter, you'll see that combining the Law of Attraction with AI isn't as strange as it seems. In the digital age, our goals, desires, and energies often show up in the data we create, the way we act online, and the digital footprints we leave. Because AI is good at recognizing patterns, it can read, understand, and react to these signals. It could become a modern way to make the Law of Attraction work better.

What if AI, with its algorithms and data, could become a friend who helped us make our goals come true more quickly? What if it could give us insights, chances, or even actions that would help us get closer to the lives we want?

Join us as we explore this fascinating place where the old and the new meet. We'll look at how the ancient Law of Attraction and cutting-edge AI can work together to give us new ways to change our lives.

Using AI to make manifestation better.

At the intersection of faith that has been around for a long time and new technology, we find a connection that is both surprising and ground-breaking. The ancient Law of Attraction is the foundation of the art of manifestation, which has always been based on being aware, visualizing, and setting intentions. But in the age of AI, we find new tools that can improve and speed up this process, allowing purpose and innovation to work together.

The Science of Getting What You Want

Before getting too deep into AI's part, it's important to understand how manifestation works from a scientific point of view. Usually, the process has three key steps: being clear about what you want, picturing what you want to happen, and aligning with the desired energy or vibe. People think that when a person has a clear vision and feels good, the universe will bring together the right people, situations, and chances to make that vision come true.

Plans and the Digital Footprint

We create a lot of data every day, whether we are aware of it or not, through the things we do online, like search engine queries, social media exchanges, and e-commerce choices. These acts often show what we want, what we hope for, and what we plan to do. Even though privacy is a valid issue, this digital footprint can be a goldmine for AI if the right steps are taken. It can help AI understand and even predict our goals.

AI: The Vision Board of Today

Think about the standard "vision board," where people put pictures, quotes, and other things that remind them of their goals. Now, picture a digital vision board that is run by AI. AI can create a personalized digital space that reinforces your goals and desires by giving you content, resources, and reminders that are in line with your vision. This is done by analyzing your interactions, search habits, and even the content you consume.

Feedback loops and getting back on track.

AI is good at giving input, which is one of its strengths. Let's say you want to get your dream job or reach a financial goal. In that case, AI can look at how you learn online, suggest courses, track your progress, and even suggest ways to network or events that fit with your goals. This creates a positive feedback loop that makes sure you don't just dream about what you want but also take steps to get what you want.

Augmented and Virtual Reality (AR and VR) for Visualization

With the rise of AR and VR, AI has made it even easier to see things. You can "experience" a desired result in a virtual space instead of just thinking about it. This makes the emotions stronger and the vision more real. For example, if you're trying to make your dream home come true,

AI-driven VR can let you walk through a model of that house, feeling the emotions and making your purpose stronger.

Aligning vibrations with meditation and mindfulness apps that use AI.

The most important part of manifestation is how it makes you feel. Apps for meditation and awareness that are powered by AI can make sessions fit your needs. For example, if you want to attract wealth, these apps can put together sessions that focus on wealth, gratitude, and success. This makes sure that your emotional vibration matches what you wan

Some Final Thoughts

AI offers strong tools to improve manifestation, but it's important to approach this in a balanced way. AI is a tool, but it can't replace the real mental and spiritual work that's needed to make things happen. It can guide, suggest, and amplify, but the core intention and energy must come from the person.

We are on the verge of a new era at this exciting point where the spiritual and the technology meet. A time when our old hopes meet new ways of doing things, when we don't just dream but also use AI to make our dreams come true. Let's move through this brave new world with purpose, honesty, and a sense of wonder.

AI offers strong tools to improve manifestation, but it's important to approach this in a balanced way. AI is a tool, but it can't replace the real mental and spiritual work that's needed to make things happen. It can guide, suggest, and amplify, but the core intention and energy must come from the person.

We are on the verge of a new era at this exciting point where the spiritual and the technology meet. A time when our old hopes meet new ways of doing things, when we don't just dream but also use AI to make our dreams come true. Let's move through this brave new world with purpose, honesty, and a sense of wonder.

Cultivating Abundance Mindset with AI Techniques

As we go through life, our way of thinking has a big impact on what we do, what happens to us, and how well we do overall. The abundance mindset is the key to achieving goals and making dreams come true. This is the belief that there is more than enough for everyone, that chances are endless, and that success is broad and includes everyone.

But how do we develop this attitude of wealth in a world that sometimes seems to focus on lack, competition, and limits? Here, combining ancient knowledge with modern Artificial Intelligence techniques gives a unique and transformative way forward.

Understanding the mindset of abundance

First, it's important to know what a "abundance mindset" looks like. A person with a scarcity mindset sees life as a zero-sum game and acts out of fear and limits. A person with an abundance mindset, on the other hand, is open to possibilities, happy for the success of others, optimistic in the face of challenges, and thinks they have unlimited potential.

AI as a Sign of Lots of Things

In a strange way, AI itself is proof of the abundance attitude. It works with huge amounts of data, finds patterns, and finds the best answers based on an infinite number of permutations and combinations. It is in its nature to sort through a lot of information to find what is important

Learning and Growth That Fits You

One of the first things you can do to develop an abundance attitude is to keep learning and improving yourself. AI-powered platforms can customize how we learn, find resources that match our interests, track our progress, and change the material based on how our needs change. Such a long, custom-made learning journey can show that there are no limits to growth and potential.

AI can be used for visualization and affirmations.

It is well known that positive affirmations and visualizing what you want can help you have an attitude of abundance. AI can make this even better by looking at our goals, likes, and even fears. Imagine an AI tool that sends you daily custom affirmations on your phone or uses AR (augmented reality) to help you see your goals, making them feel more real and attainable.

Mindset shifts can be tracked and given feedback.

Getting rid of thoughts and actions that are based on scarcity is an important part of having an abundance mindset. AI can gently let us know when we're leaning toward negativity or self-limiting beliefs by analyzing the tone of our digital conversations or journal entries. It can also offer resources or prompts to get us back to a mindset of abundance.

Meditation and mindfulness that are powered by AI

Several apps that are driven by AI now offer guided meditations that help you develop a positive, grateful, and abundant mindset. By getting feedback on our moods, responses, and tastes, these apps can keep improving their advice and make sure we get the most out of each session.

Building up a community and AI

One part of an abundance mindset that is often ignored is the community part, which means celebrating the successes of others and surrounding yourself with positive, like-minded people. AI can help with this by putting us in touch with online communities, platforms, or groups that share our goals. This creates a sense of abundance for everyone.

Conclusion

When you combine AI methods with a mindset of wanting more, you can look forward to a bright future. The most important thing about tools is how we use them. AI can be a strong ally for someone who wants to improve themselves and see the good in the world. As we use these methods, it's important to keep the human part in mind and make sure that even though we're using advanced algorithms and technologies, the heart's core beliefs and goals are still based on abundance.

Chapter 3: Aligning Values and Goals

Identifying Core Values: Ancient Insights and AI Tools

Every person's quest for success and happiness starts with figuring out what their core ideals are. These values are like driving principles that help us decide what to do, how to act, and how our lives should go. Ancient knowledge has long given us clues about how to think about these values and figure out what they mean to us. Now, with the rise of AI, we have new tools to improve and add to this age-old quest.

Core values don't change over time.

Since ancient times, educators, religious leaders, and other thinkers have stressed how important it is to know what your core values are. These are the truths and ideas that don't change and give our lives meaning. They help us find our way when we're not sure what to do and shape how we react to the world around us.

- **How Ancient People Found Their Core Values**

- Several ancient methods were made to help people think about themselves and find these guiding principles:

- Meditation is a deep state of thought that helps people get away from outside distractions and connect with their inner selves.

- Journaling is the practice of writing down your thoughts, feelings, and memories. Over time, this can be like a mirror for your soul.

- Guided introspection: This is often done with the help of a wise person or guru, and it includes deep conversations, questions, and thoughts about one's inner world

- **AI Tools: The Modern Way to Look Inside Yourself**

- In the digital age we live in now, AI gives us a new viewpoint and a set of tools to help us find our core values:

- **Sentiment analysis:** By looking at our digital footprints, like social media posts, texts, and emails, AI can find patterns, tastes, and values that we may express unconsciously.

- **Journals with AI**: Modern journaling apps can ask users questions that are meant to make them think, based on their previous entries and trends they have noticed.

- **Scenarios for Virtual Reality (VR)**: VR can put people in different simulated scenarios. AI can look at how people respond and what they choose to do in these situations to figure out what their values are.

- **Feedback and recognizing patterns**: AI can give us feedback on our daily decisions, actions, and relationships by pointing out patterns that align with our core values.

Bringing together the old and the new

- AI tools give us new and efficient ways to learn about our values, but it's important to make sure that these findings are based on real self-awareness. Here's how to combine the two in a way that works well:

- se old methods like meditation and writing in a diary to develop a deep sense of self-awareness.

- Use AI tools to improve this learning by giving you insights and patterns based on data.

- Look at AI-based insights through the lens of self-reflection on a regular basis to make sure they match your real feelings and beliefs.

- Leave room for growth and change. Even though core beliefs are important, they are not set in stone. Both old knowledge and information from AI should be used as guides, not as hard rules

Conclusion

The process of figuring out what your core ideals are is deeply personal and changes you. By combining the deep insights of ancient knowledge with the analytical power of AI tools, people can find a balanced, complete, and changing understanding of their guiding principles. This, in turn, is the foundation for aligning goals and moving through life with focus and purpose.

Setting goals with the help of AI clarity

Setting clear, doable goals is the first step toward making your dreams and goals come true. People have been looking for ways to make their goals clear and make sure they match their core values and goals for hundreds of years. Today, when tradition and technology meet, we have the benefit of being able to combine ancient wisdom about setting goals with the accuracy of Artificial Intelligence. This gives us a level of clarity that was previously unimaginable.

How people used to set goals

Philosophers, scholars, and successful people have all talked about how important it is to set clear goals throughout history. Ancient techniques have always been about looking inward, visualizing what we want, and making our deepest wishes come true.

Visualization: From ancient cultures to current psychology, seeing the end result in your mind has always been a key part. Even if it's just in your mind, seeing your goals come true is a strong push toward making them come true.

Scripting: People in many countries have always thought that writing down their goals helped them reach them. With this actual action, an idea turns into a real goal.

Accountability: In the past, people often worked together toward common goals and made progress as a group. When someone in such a group said what they were going to do, they were held accountable

The role of AI in setting and reaching goals

In the digital age we live in now, AI gives us a lot of tools that can make our goals clearer and help us reach them:

Data-Driven Insights: AI can sort through a huge amount of data from many different sources to find trends, options, and paths to success that are best for each person.

Customized Roadmaps: AI can make customized goal-setting roadmaps based on a person's past accomplishments, behaviors, and patterns, breaking down big goals into steps that can be taken.

Progress Tracking: AI tools can keep an eye on a person's progress toward their goals and give them feedback, help them change their path, and keep them going.

Scenario Analysis: AI can model different ways to reach a goal by using advanced algorithms to show possible challenges and opportunities. This lets a person choose the best way to reach the goal.

Putting together the old and the new

When you combine the depth of old methods with the accuracy of AI, you can set goals with more clarity than ever before:

Start by thinking about yourself and using age-old methods like visualizing and writing to figure out what you really want.

Use AI tools to turn these vague wishes into clear goals that can be done. Let the algorithms, which are based on data-driven insights, show the range of options.

AI can help you keep track of your work and make sure you stay on track. Take advantage of the fact that technology can suggest course changes when they are needed.Always come back to thinking about yourself. Make sure that the ideas made by AI fit with your values and the way you want your life to go.

Conclusion

Setting goals is an art that changes over time. Human desire and drive are still at the heart of it, but the tools we use to reach our goals have grown and changed. By combining the wisdom of the ancients with the power of AI, we can see our way more clearly than ever before, making sure that our goals are not only clear but also deeply in line with who we really are.

Harmonizing Values and Goals for Lasting Wealth

In its many forms, trying to get rich isn't just about collecting things. When a person's core values are in line with their wealth, they feel it strongly. This kind of alignment turns temporary wins into lasting legacies. Not only what you do matters, but also how and why you do it. As we go through this chapter, we'll talk about the deep art of matching values with goals to make sure that our efforts lead to wealth that lasts.

The Long-Term Importance of Values in Making Money

Through stories, teachings, and customs, every culture has shown how important values are for making and keeping wealth. From the stories of old Indian merchants to the parables of the Bible, the message is always the same: wealth that goes against your own values is temporary.

Inner Satisfaction: Money that reflects your ideals doesn't just take care of your material needs; it also takes care of your spiritual and emotional needs.

Building a legacy: Material wealth can be lost in one generation, but when it's tied to values, it becomes a heritage that can be passed on to the next generation with stories, lessons, and a name that sticks.

When you let your values lead your pursuit of wealth, they act as a shield during economic downturns, market uncertainty, and personal challenges. They help people be strong, patient, and able to change.

Modern Goals and the Danger of Contradiction

In the modern world, there are so many options that our goals and ideals can sometimes become different. The constant chase of modern goals, which is often caused by pressures from society, can lead to

Short-term Gains: When people focus on short-term gains, they often don't think about the long-term effects, which can lead to temporary success.

Dissatisfaction: Even if you reach your goals, you might still feel empty if they don't match up with your values.

Burnouts and mental strain: Trying to do things that go against your own values can cause stress, burnout, and a lower sense of self-worth.

Bringing harmony: Bridging the Gap

With intention and awareness, it is possible to make sure that modern goals are in line with ideals that have been around for a long time:

Every so often, you should think about yourself and your goals. Not only should you question the "what" of your goals, but also the "why." Learn as much as you can about what drives you to do what you do.

Stakeholder's Point of View: Think about how your ways of making money affect your family, neighborhood, employees, and even the environment. This big-picture view makes sure that ideals like empathy, care, and sustainability are in line.

Use technology to help with alignment. Modern tools, especially AI, can help track alignment. They can keep an eye on choices, investments, and actions and give feedback if they seem to be getting away from the company's core values.

Find a mentor. Spend time with people who have a good balance of ideals and money. Their experiences, advice, and ideas can be very helpful guides.

Conclusion

Lasting wealth isn't just about how much money someone has in the bank. It's also about how well their assets and who they fit together. By making sure that our values drive our goals, we create a road to prosperity that is satisfying, lasts, and serves as a light for future generations.

Chapter 4: Practical Ways to Create Wealth for Families

Navigating Family Finances with Ancient Wisdom

How to Handle Family Finances with Help from the Past

Making money is not a new idea. For hundreds of years, families have tried to make sure their relatives are financially stable. This drive to make and keep money has led to a lot of information, especially from ancient civilizations, that can be used to plan for money today. Let's look at some timeless ways to handle family finances that come from old knowledge.

Confucius said, "Live within your means."

Confucius, an old Chinese philosopher, once said, "He who does not save money will have to suffer." This shows how important it is to spend less than you make. For families, this can mean making a budget, cutting costs where they aren't needed, and saving regularly.

Don't get into debt: Hammurabi's Code

Under King Hammurabi, the ancient Babylonians knew how dangerous it was to be in debt. His code was one of the first sets of laws. It had rules about giving and borrowing that kept people from getting into too much debt. Families shouldn't take on too much debt and should try to pay off their debts as soon as possible.

Invest in different things - The Story of the Talents

In an old Bible story from the Book of Matthew, a master gave his workers "talents," which are coins. Diversifying their assets and taking calculated risks paid off. Modern families can learn from this and protect themselves from market downturns by investing in a variety of assets.

Land was a valuable asset for the ancient Egyptians

Land was important to the ancient Egyptians not only for farming, but also as a sign of wealth and power. Real estate is still a tried-and-true way to invest today. Whether you live in the house or rent it out, it can be a source of passive income and capital appreciation.

The Power of Compounding: Indian Wisdom from the Past

The idea of interest that grows over time can be found in old Indian texts. The idea that money grows by a factor of ten when it is re-invested can be very helpful for families. Start saving early and put back the money you earn to get the most growth.

Being Ready for an Emergency: Joseph in Egypt

The story in the Bible about Joseph figuring out what Pharaoh's dream meant and telling him to save food for seven years to get ready for seven years of famine is an early example of how to get ready for things you don't know will happen. Families should save money in case they have to pay for something unexpected.

Teaching About Values: Ancient Greece

The ancient Greeks valued information and thought that learning should be about the whole person. Families should invest in their children's education today, and not just in the classroom. They should also help their kids learn about money, how to think critically, and other life skills.

Ancient African customs about community and giving.

A lot of African groups believe in Ubuntu, which means "I am because we are." It shows how important community and the well-being of everyone is. Families can do well if they invest in their communities, help others, and realize that their own success is tied to the success of the society

Conclusion:

Even though the financial world has changed over thousands of years, the rules for making and keeping money haven't changed. By putting these ancient pearls of financial knowledge into practice today, families can deal with the complicated world we live in and make sure that future generations will be prosperous.

Budgeting for Families with AI

As the digital age moves forward quickly, families now have more ways to budget and plan their finances. AI is at the forefront of this change, helping families better handle their money with solutions that are accurate, easy to use, and often automated. Here's how families can use AI to make their budgets better:

An introduction to AI in budgeting: AI uses algorithms and machine learning to quickly look at big data sets. When used in personal finance, AI can sort through a huge number of transactions and financial habits to give you insights, predictions, and steps you can take to make your family's budget work better.

Automatic tracking of expenses: Gone are the days when you had to type in every cost by hand into a spreadsheet. Modern budgeting apps are powered by artificial intelligence (AI) and can instantly group and track expenses from linked accounts. This gives families a real-time look at how they spend their money.

Predictive budgeting: AI can predict future costs by looking at how people have spent money in the past. This helps families get ready for upcoming financial obligations. Predictive budgeting can make a big difference for families, whether it's figuring out the next month's energy bill or preparing for a big expense.

Personalized Savings Strategies: AI tools look at how you handle your money and offer ways for you to save money that are unique to you. AI can help people save money by helping them cut back on eating out, find cheaper choices for recurring costs, or find subscriptions that aren't being used

Plans for paying off debt: AI can help families with debt come up with the best way to pay it back. AI can figure out the best way to pay less interest and get out of debt faster by looking at interest rates, amounts owed, and the family's financial situation.

Investment Insights: AI can help families make smart investment choices, but it's not a direct budgeting tool. AI can help families figure out where to spend their money to get the best return by predicting market trends based on huge amounts of data.

Setting interactive financial goals: Many AI-powered budgeting tools let families set financial goals, like saving for a trip, buying a home, or building an emergency fund. The AI then helps you keep track of your progress and offers changes to make it easier to reach your goals.

Security and privacy: AI tools put the safety of user data first. With advanced encryption and security measures, families can be sure that their financial information stays private and is safe from possible breaches.

Educational Resources: Many AI budgeting platforms include educational resources that are made to fit the wants and habits of the user. These could be things like articles, videos, or interactive simulations about how to save, trade, or deal with debt, which would help families learn more about money over time.

Conclusion

AI has powerful tools for budgeting, but it's important for families to stay involved in their money choices. AI should be used as a helper, not as an alternative. Families can have a financially stable and successful future by combining the computing power of AI with human reasoning and family values.

Building wealth together for the success of many generations

Building wealth isn't just one person's job; it's a family project that involves people from different groups. A strong base built by one generation can help the next generation do well, and so on. Let's talk about how families can work together to build wealth that will last for many generations.

The Importance of Leaving a Legacy:

Thinking about leaving a legacy isn't just about giving things to the next generation; it's also about passing on principles, knowledge, and a sense of responsibility. Families need to realize that what they do now will affect the chances and problems of the next generation.

Open Lines of Communication:

The first step to building wealth across generations is to talk openly about money, beliefs, goals, and responsibilities. By making it easy for people to talk about money, families can make sure that their financial goals are the same from one generation to the next.

Teaching all ages about money:

The older generation might know how to save and spend in the traditional way, while the younger generation might know more about digital assets, modern investment vehicles, and tech-based financial tools. By sharing this information, the family as a whole can learn more about money.

Investments and joint ventures:

Family members can work together instead of on their own to invest in bigger, more profitable businesses. This not only brings in more money, but also makes people feel like they are all in it together.

Diversification of investments:

Based on where they are in life and how well they understand the market, each group has its own risk tolerance. By putting these different ideas together, families can make an investment portfolio that has a good mix of risk and return.

Planning your will:

One of the most important parts of building wealth across generations is making sure that assets are passed on with as little loss as possible due to taxes and legal issues. With the help of pros, proper estate planning can make sure that things go smoothly.

Taking advantage of technological advances:

Older people might swear by traditional banks, but younger people might be more interested in fintech solutions and digital assets like cryptocurrencies. By looking at and using these tools together, you can make a more solid financial plan.

Giving to charity and being responsible for the community:

Giving back is another way to build wealth. By setting up charitable trusts or doing community work, families can n   ot   only   pass   on their wealth, but they may also get tax breaks and build a better name for themselves.

Creating "soft assets":

Soft assets like schooling, skills, business sense, and networks are just as important as financial assets. By encouraging each generation to get and improve these assets, the family's ability to build wealth can be increased.

Getting ready for the unexpected:

There are a lot of unknowns in life. Families with more than one generation should work together to make backup plans so that unplanned events don't ruin the family's financial future. This could include things like insurance, a disaster fund, and legal protections.

Conclusion

Building wealth over many generations isn't just about money; it's a sign of a family's beliefs, foresight, and unity as well. By working together, families can make sure that their memory isn't just about money, but also about hard work, being smart, and taking care of each other. Every age has a unique part to play in this journey, and every person has something to teach and learn

Chapter 5: The Ancient Law of Giving and Receiving

The Ancient Law of Giving and Receiving

Civilizations and nations all over the world have talked about how important it is to give and receive. This continuous flow not only keeps society together, but it also helps people find their way spiritually and morally. Let's look at what ancient people knew about this general law.

Understanding the Cycle: Giving and getting is a cycle, not a one-time thing. Ancient people knew about this balance. When you give, you make room to receive, and when you receive, it makes you want to give more.

Ancient Texts and Scriptures:

The Vedas (Hinduism): The ancient Indian texts often support the idea of "Dana," or charity, where giving without expecting anything in return leads to spiritual and material success.

"It is more blessed to give than to receive" (Acts 20:35), which is in the Bible, says what Christianity is all about: giving without expecting anything in return.

In Islam, the Quran: Charity, or "Zakat," is one of the Five Pillars of Islam. It stresses that giving some of your money to people who need it will make you rich.

Tao Te Ching (Taoism): This text talks about how good it is to give without expecting anything in return. It says that this is the way of the Tao, or the basic nature of the world.

The ideas and beliefs of ancient societies:

In ancient Egypt, the idea of Ma'at was all about unity and balance. It suggested that giving helps keep the universe and society in balance.

In ancient Greece, the act of giving, called "Charis," was thought to create a link between the giver and the receiver, with obligations and benefits for both sides. This strengthened the social cohesion of the community.

The Law of Reciprocity: This is an old idea that says when you help someone, the world will help you back in the future, even if it's not from the person you helped. It's the idea that being kind and generous causes a chain reaction that comes back to the person who started it.

Empowering the Giver and the Receiver: In ancient times, both the giver and the receiver were thought to be important. Giving was never about being better than someone else, and getting was never about being worse. Both acts were seen as holy and important for the growth of society and the spiritual growth of each person.

Festivals and traditions: From the potlatch ceremonies of the native groups of the Pacific Northwest to the Diwali festival in India, cultures all over the world have days that focus on giving to show how important it is to people's lives.

Physical and spiritual returns: It's clear that giving has physical benefits, like getting gifts or favors in return, but ancient advice focuses on the spiritual benefits. Kindness and acts of charity were thought to cleanse the soul and bring a person closer to God.

Modern Implications: Today's acts of kindness and philanthropy are based on ancient knowledge. Even though the methods have changed, the core ideas have not: give without expecting anything in return, accept with grace, and keep things in balance.

In Conclusion:

The ancient wisdom of giving and getting isn't just about making money; it's also a way of thinking that, if you follow it, can help you live a full and balanced life. It shows us that wealth isn't just about accumulating things, but also about moving things around. As we learn more about these ancient lessons, it becomes clear that embracing this cyclical flow can help us grow as individuals, as a society, and as spiritual beings.

Impactful Giving through AI

Getting starte

In this digital age that is always changing, Artificial Intelligence (AI) has changed many fields, from healthcare to banking. Philanthropy and giving to charity are no different. By using AI's capabilities, people, organizations, and governments can make their gifts have a bigger effect and make sure that every dollar goes to the right place.

Giving based on data:

One of the best things about AI is that it can examine a lot of data quickly and effectively. This lets donors know where their money can make the most difference by pointing out places that aren't getting enough help or new crises that need attention.

Giving with a personal touch:

AI can find chances for donors based on their interests, how much they've given in the past, and what the world needs. This is similar to how AI customizes online shopping or streaming recommendations. This makes sure that donors feel closer to the causes they give money to.

Predictive analysis for managing crises:

AI can be used to identify natural disasters, economic downturns, and health pandemics. AI can help donors decide where to put their money ahead of time by looking for patterns. This way, when a problem happens, help will be there quickly.

Making administrative tasks easier to do:

One thing that people don't like about charities is that some of the money they get is used to run the group. AI can take care of many of these jobs automatically, making sure that more of the money goes to the people who need it.

Making things more open and trustworthy:

AI-powered platforms can show how donations are being used in real time by tracking the flow of money and showing the effect on the ground. Knowing that their donations are making a difference can make more people want to help out.

How to tell if a charity is a scam:

Unfortunately, not all groups that do-good things are real. AI can be used to check out and vet groups, making sure that donors don't fall for scams.

Getting new donors to give:

With AI chatbots and interactive platforms, younger generations who are tech-savvy can be introduced to charity in a way that makes sense to them. This will increase the number of people who give money to charities.

Giving with the help of AI networks:

Imagine a network where many donors can work together and pool their resources based on AI suggestions to solve big problems. This kind of cooperation can make each person's input more powerful.

Feedback and learning all the time:

AI works best when it gets input. By looking at how different charity projects turned out, these systems can improve their suggestions and make giving more effective in the future.

Longevity and long-term effects:

Instead of just helping with instant problems, AI can point donors toward projects that will help in the long run. For example, instead of just giving money to feed the hungry, AI might suggest giving money to a farming project that makes sure there will always be food.

In Conclusion

AI can change the way people give to charity if it is used in an ethical and effective way. Even though empathy and compassion are unique to humans and can't be replaced, AI can help make sure that this kindness is used in the most effective way. As technology keeps getting better, the combination of AI and giving back to the community offers a brighter, more hopeful future for everyone

Building Abundance through Universal Generosity

Building abundance by giving to everyone

Introduction

Giving without expecting anything in return is the essence of generosity. This idea is taken a step further by the idea of universal generosity, which says that when people, communities, and countries are all generous, it makes it easier for everyone to have enough. This chapter goes into detail about how a global method to giving can make a lot of people rich.

1. **The Cycle of Generosity and Abundance:** When generosity is followed by everyone, it creates a culture of giving and receiving. This cycle not only makes people better off, but it also makes communities stronger by making an ecosystem where resources flow easily and everyone benefits.

2. **Breaking the "scarcity mindset":** The fear of not having enough is a big reason why people don't give as much as they could. Societies can move from a mindset of scarcity to one of wealth by realizing that having a lot of resources doesn't always mean hoarding them, but sharing and moving them around.

3. **Economic Effects of Universal Generosity**: When groups and countries put a priority on being generous, it can lead to a better distribution of wealth and a decrease in extreme economic differences. This not only makes people's lives better, but it can also help the economy grow because more people will be able to take part in it.

4. **Bringing the world closer together**: Generosity around the world brings people closer together. When countries help each other out in times of trouble or support development projects in poorer countries, it makes international relationships better, which leads to a more peaceful world.

5. **Using technology to help people be more generous:** In the digital age, technology is a strong tool that can help everyone be more generous. Crowdfunding sites, global charity efforts, and even blockchain technology can be used to make sure that resources are shared around the world in a transparent and efficient way.

6. **Taking care of the environment:** Being generous isn't just about sharing things. By practicing sustainability and being kind to our planet, we can make sure that future generations will have a world full of resources.

7. **The happiness and well-being of each person**: Studies have shown over and over that people who are kind tend to be happier and more satisfied with their lives. Societies can improve the well-being of their people as a whole by encouraging a culture of generosity.

8. **The Role of Education:** For universal charity to work well, it's important to teach people about its benefits from a young age. Schools, community centers, and even online platforms can teach about the ideas of generosity and wealth through classes and workshops.

9. **Generosity in Government:** When governments put generosity at the center of their policies, whether through foreign help, welfare programs, or community development projects, it can make the whole country stronger and more prosperous.

10. **Spirituality and Generosity:** Around the world, many spiritual groups stress how important it is to be kind. By learning and accepting these teachings, people can find a deeper, more meaningful reason to be kind to everyone.

In Conclusion

Giving to everyone isn't just a nice thought for a perfect world. It's a realistic goal that can be reached with teamwork, a change in attitude, and the right tools and plans. When societies, communities, and people come together under this banner of universal generosity, it opens the way for a world where plenty is not the privilege of a few but the right of all.

Chapter 6: Ancient Principles of Mindfulness and Abundance

Ancient Principles of Mindfulness and Abundance

Introduction

Mindfulness is often thought of as a modern buzzword, but it has its roots in old practices. These traditions, which come from many different cultures and religions, have often tied being mindful to not only material but also emotional and spiritual wealth.

An Old Way to Get Rich and Be Mindful

1. **The Basics of Mindfulness:** At its core, mindfulness is about being fully present in the moment, without distractions, and in tune with oneself and one's surroundings. This doesn't just mean having a lot of money. It also means having a lot of knowledge, understanding, and compassion.

"Don't think about the past and don't dream about the future. Keep your mind on the present." — Buddhism

2. **Buddhist Teachings on Mindfulness and Abundance:** The Buddhist practice of "Satipatthana," or the foundations of mindfulness, focuses on watching the body, feelings, mind, and dhammas. By doing this, you can find peace inside, which will lead to a lot of kindness and understanding.

The Satipatthana Sutta tells us everything we need to know about how to practice awareness.

3. Hinduism from the point of view of the Bhagavad Gita:

The Hindu holy book Bhagavad Gita talks about "Dhyana," which is another word for meditation. Here, Lord Krishna tells Arjuna that being aware and meditating are great ways to find peace inside.

"A person can only find peace if they are not bothered by the constant flow of desires, which are like rivers flowing into an ocean that is always full but always still. The person who tries to satisfy these desires will never find peace." -- The Bhagavad Gita

4. Taoism and the Way of Being: Taoism focuses on the "Way" or "Tao," which is a road of balance and harmony. Here, wealth isn't about collecting things. Instead, it's about going with the natural flow of life, which leads to real riches.

"Be happy with what you have and happy with how things are. When you understand you have everything you need, the whole world is yours." — Tao Te Ching by Lao Tzu

5. Christianity and Mindful Stewardship: Different parts of the Bible teach Christians to be good stewards of the Earth's wealth. In this case, abundance is about being thankful and making good use of what you have.

"So do not worry, saying, 'What shall we eat?' or 'What shall we drink?' or 'What shall we wear?'" But first seek his kingdom and his justice, and you will get all these other things as well. Matthew 6:31 to 33

6. Sufism and the Wealth of the Heart: Sufism is an Islamic mystical practice that focuses on the purity of the heart and a direct experience with the Divine. Here, there is a lot of love and understanding from God.

"The universe is not somewhere else. Look inside yourself; you already have everything you want." — Rumi

Traditional Wisdom and Mindful Living: Many indigenous cultures around the world stress living in harmony with nature, understanding its rhythms, and being aware of every resource, seeing them as gifts.

"We do not inherit the earth from our ancestors, we borrow it from our children." — An old Native American saying

Conclusion

In our fast-paced world, the old ideas of being present and having enough are good reminders. These teachings, which come from many different cultures and times, help us get a better understanding of what it means to be wealthy. They push us to look beyond material things and embrace the wealth that comes from awareness, understanding, and inner peace.

Abundance Mindset with AI-Powered Meditation

Introduction

The idea of an abundance mindset and the rise of AI-powered meditation tools have become the most important things in terms of both mental health and technical progress. When these things come together, they create opportunities for personal growth and satisfaction that are unmatched.

Getting a grasp on the "abundance mindset"

Before getting into how AI and meditation work together, it's important to know what a "abundance mindset" is. This point of view moves the attention away from scarcity, or the fear that there isn't enough, and toward the belief that there are no limits to what can be done. It's about believing that there's enough for everyone and seeing the many possibilities around us.

"The mind is all there is. "You become what you think." — Buddhism

The Rise of Meditation Tools that Use AI

Meditation is easier to do now because of technology, especially AI. AI meditation apps offer personalized advice by looking at the user's preferences, habits, and responses. This makes meditation less of a generic practice and more of a personalized journey.

Making your own path to wealth

Because AI is so good at analyzing, meditation sessions can be changed on the fly to help people develop a "abundance mindset." AI can help people see the world in a more open and expansive way by suggesting guided visualizations that focus on gratitude or giving feedback on meditation methods.

Keeping track of progress and changing plans

One big benefit of AI-powered meditation is that you can keep track of your progress over time. By tracking things like heart rate, breathing patterns, or even how you feel during meditation, AI tools can change their methods to help you have a better abundance mindset.

Connectivity around the world and shared wealth

Adding AI to meditation could also make it easier to meet people all over the world. AI can bring together meditators from all over the world, making it easier for them to hold group meditations that focus on global wealth, unity, and collective prosperity.

"Alone, we can do so little; together, we can do so much." — Henrietta Lacks

AI Feedback Can Help You Get Past Limiting Beliefs

AI's ability to analyze data can show trends, which could point to deeply held limiting beliefs. The first step toward changing from a mindset of lack to one of plenty is to become aware of these trends.

Learning and changing all the time

the AI, which keeps giving them new techniques, insights, and advice to help them develop a deeper attitude of abundance.

Implications for the Future: More Than Just Meditation

Even though the use of AI in meditation right now is new, the future looks even better. We might see AI- powered virtual realities made for meditation that increase the feeling of wealth or even AI-led spiritual retreats that are customized to each person's spiritual and mental growth paths.

Conclusion

When you combine an abundance mindset with AI-powered meditation, you can go on a journey that changes you. It shows how old practices and modern technology can work together to create paths to holistic health and a deeper understanding of the world's many opportunities. When we embrace this synergy, we can move into a future where wealth is not just a way of thinking, but a way of life.

Balancing Present and Financial Future

Introduction

In the complicated dance of life, one of the hardest steps is to find a balance between immediate wants and long-term goals. In terms of money, this means living easily now while making sure you have a safe future. This part goes into the plans and ways of thinking that are needed to find this delicate balance.

1.   Finding a Good Balance

Getting your finances in order doesn't just mean dividing funds. It's about lining up one's present choices with goals for the future. Living only for today can put tomorrow at risk, but saving every bit could mean missing out on the pleasures of today.

"Do not save what is left over after spending but spend what is left over after saving." — Warren

Buffet

2.   The Foundation: Learning about money

Before you can find a good balance, you need to know the basics of personal spending. This includes knowing how to make a budget, invest, pay off bills, and save money. If you have a strong base, you can make good choices.

3.   Planning your budget for today and tomorrow

Putting together a budget isn't just about keeping track of spending. It's a tool for making plans, like putting money aside for current needs and goals for the future. By sticking to a well-organized budget, one can live easily while also building a nest egg.

4.   The Power of Interest That Builds Up

Understanding compound interest and using it to your advantage can change your life. It shows that even a small amount of money can grow very quickly if it is spent wisely over time. This theory shows how important it is to start saving and investing early on.

5.   Living with What You Have

One way to find a balance between the present and the future is to not take on too much debt. Mortgages and student loans can be thought of as investments for the future, but high-interest credit card debt from making hasty purchases can be bad.

6.   Set clear goals for your money

Having clear, well-defined financial goals for the future, like retirement, buying a home, or paying for your children's schooling, can help you decide how to spend your money now. It helps you see what's really important today and what you can give up for the goals of tomorrow.

7.   Taking a minimalist approach

Minimalism isn't about living with as little as possible; it's about putting what's most important first. By putting more value on events and necessities than on things, one can find happiness in the present while also making sure their financial future is safe.

"It's not the daily increase but daily decrease. Hack away at the unessential." — Bruce Lee

8.   Ongoing education about money

The world of money is always changing. It is important to keep up with market changes, new business opportunities, and changes in the economy. Continuous learning not only helps a person get richer, but it also protects them from money problems.

9.   Start a fund in case of an emergency

Getting ready for the unknown is an important part of balancing the present and the future. An emergency fund works as a safety net, making sure that unplanned events don't throw off long-term financial plans.

10. Looking for Advice

Financial advisors can sometimes help people find the right mix. These experts can come up with plans that fit each person's income, spending habits, and goals for the future.

Conclusion

Finding a good balance between the present and the future in terms of money is an ongoing process that takes awareness, focus, and consistent effort. It's about appreciating what today has to offer and keeping the promises of tomorrow. By using the methods and ways of thinking that are talked about in this chapter, you can find your way to a happy present and a successful future.

Chapter 7: AI-Driven Insights into Cause and Effect

Exploring Ancient Wisdom on Cause and Effect Predictive Financial Analysis with AI

Mastering Outcomes through Informed Decisions

Exploring Ancient Wisdom on Cause and Effect

Introduction

Cause and effect is an old intellectual idea that has been studied and talked about in many different places and times. Many spiritual and philosophical systems stress how important this principle is, but artificial intelligence has given us new ways to study and understand this very old idea. This part gives a nuanced look at how the old and the new can work together.

What Ancient People Knew About Cause and Effect

1.   The ideas that stand behind it

Many philosophical systems are based on the idea that every action has an equal and opposite reaction. The basic idea is the same whether it is called "karma" in Hinduism and Buddhism or "cause and effect" in Western thinking.

"Every action has equal and opposite reactions." — Sir Isaac Newton

2.   Karma and Rebirth: Two Ancient Eastern Ideas

Hinduism and Buddhism talk about karma, which is the idea that actions have moral consequences that affect a person's fate in this life or the next. People think that good actions lead to good results and bad actions lead to bad results.

The Bhagavad Gita says, "As we sow, so shall we reap," which is a way of saying that our deeds will always have consequences.

3.   Western Philosophies: Why Things Happen the Way They Do

From the ancient Greeks to the thinkers of the Enlightenment, people in the West have been interested in how causes lead to results. Both philosophy and physics have been built on this idea.

"Man is free when he wants to be," says this quote. Voltaire said that even though people have free will, they have to live with the results of their choices.

How the Web is Connected

Indigenous people all over the world see the universe as a web of connections. From this point of view, every action, no matter how small, influences other parts of the system that might not be clear at first.

"Walk softly on the Earth, because everything is connected, and you are just one thread in the web." — American Indian saying.

AI-based insights into what causes what.

4. Machine Learning and Recognition of Patterns

Through machine learning, modern AI is able to look at huge amounts of data, find patterns, and make connections that a person might miss. This shows how certain acts (causes) can lead to certain results (effects) in a new way.

5. Analytics for the future

AI can predict what might happen in the future based on what has happened in the past. Such information is very helpful in fields like finance, health care, and climate modeling because it lets people make choices that are well-informed and consider possible outcomes.

6. What AI predictions mean for ethics

But there are ethical problems with depending only on AI to figure out what will happen and why? Bias in the data can lead to unfair results, the continuation of stereotypes, or unfair ways of doing things. It is important to recognize and deal with these biases.

"Ethics, fairness, and the rules of justice don't change with the date on the calendar." — D.H.

Reinforcement Learning: AI that knows what causes what

In reinforcement learning, AI systems learn the best thing to do based on rewards or punishments, which is a basic way of knowing cause and effect. Such programs can make decisions based on what might happen.

Conclusion

Ancient knowledge and modern AI-driven insights into cause and effect help us understand this timeless concept in a deep way. AI gives us tools to analyze, predict, and learn from huge amounts of data, but ancient philosophies give us the moral and spiritual structure to make sense of these insights and act on them in a responsible way. Together, they show how our world is made up of a complicated dance of actions and results.

Predictive Financial Analysis with AI

Introduction

Artificial intelligence (AI) is leading a change in the business world that has never happened before. Predictive financial analysis used to be based on human intuition and complicated formulas. Now, AI makes it faster, more accurate, and easier to change. In this chapter, we'll look at how AI has changed the field of predictive financial analysis.

Why predictive analysis is important in finance

In finance, predictive analysis means looking at past data to predict future financial trends, like how the stock market will move or how well a company will do. Investors, financial planners, and business managers can benefit a lot from this kind of foresight.

"It's not the strongest species that survives, and it's not the smartest species that survives, either. It is the one that can adapt to change the best." Charles Darwin. This idea fits with how the financial markets are always changing.

AI: It Will Change Everything

AI goes beyond standard ways of analyzing finances because it can process very large datasets very quickly. Machine learning is a type of AI that can find trends that humans might not be able to see.

Neural networks and making predictions about money

Deep learning neural networks, which are based on the way the human brain works, can recognize complex patterns. In the world of business, this means that stock prices, market changes, and economic trends can be predicted more accurately.

Financial Analysis and Natural Language Processing (NLP)

NLP is another part of AI that looks at how people talk. In finance, it looks at news stories, financial reports, and social media to get a sense of how the market feels, which can help predict how the market might move.

Analytics in real time and making decisions

AI's ability to handle data in real time makes it possible to make decisions right away. This means that high-frequency traders and financial institutions need to use real-time analytics to make investment choices in a split second.

AI and Risk Management

AI helps make it easier to figure out how dangerous something is. By looking at the state of the market, how well a company is doing, and what's going on in the world, AI can create a complete risk profile. This lets people make safer and more informed decisions.

Concerns about ethics and AI in finance

AI has a lot of benefits, but it also raises moral questions. To make sure AI is used fairly and responsibly, problems like data privacy, lack of openness in AI decision-making, and possible biases in AI algorithms need to be solved.

"With great power comes great responsibility." — French philosopher Voltaire. This idea is very important as we give AI more freedom in making business decisions.

What's next for financial forecasting?

When quantum computing, more advanced AI algorithms, and international data all come together, it will change the way that predictive financial analysis is done even more. As AI systems get smarter, they will be able to make even more complex and accurate predictions about the economy.

Conclusion

When AI and predictive financial research come together, it's the start of a new era in finance. It promises better predictions, the ability to make decisions in real time, and a better knowledge of global financial trends. But with these improvements comes the need to use such strong tools in a responsible way, so that everyone's financial future is open, honest, and fair.

Mastering Outcomes through Informed Decisions

Introduction

Our lives, businesses, and communities are all shaped by decisions, both big and small. When we make decisions based on facts, we don't just react to events; instead, we shape them. This chapter will talk about how important it is to make decisions based on good information and how that has a big effect on getting what you want.

The Parts of Making Decisions

When we know how choices are made, we can be more deliberate and well-informed. Most decisions include the following:

Raw facts and facts that have been understood are both types of data. Emotions and intuition are gut feelings and behaviors that come naturally. Values and beliefs are the rules and ideas that guide decisions"

Life is a series of decisions made with incomplete information, and if we waited to clear up all our doubts, it would pass us by." — Taught Hand

How important it is to know things.

In the computer age, data is all around us. But it's important to know the difference between facts and useful, actionable information:

Quantitative vs. Qualitative Data: Knowing how to use both numbers and words to describe

data.

Relevance: Making sure the knowledge fits with the choice that needs to be made. Reliability: Making sure that info sources are real and correct.

Emotional smarts and making decisions

While facts are what drive choices, emotions help explain them. Emotional intelligence, which is the ability to notice, understand, and control our own feelings, is very important:

Self-awareness means being aware of your own feelings and preferences.

Empathy is taking into account the feelings and points of view of those who will be affected by a choice.

"Your emotions are slaves to your thoughts, and you are the slave to your emotions." — Author Elizabeth Gilbert

Using technology to make smart choices

Modern technologies, particularly AI, play an important role in making decisions:

Predictive analysis is figuring out what might happen based on what has happened in the past.

Real-time data processing is the use of current information to make choices right away. Simulation models involve making stories to figure out what will happen.

The moral side of making decisions

Every choice has consequences. It's important to think about the moral implications:

Transparency means being honest about why choices were made. Accountability is being responsible for your choices and how they turn out.

"Ethics is knowing the difference between what is right and what you have the right to do." —

P. Stewart Potter

Looking back and making changes: the feedback loop

Feedback is an important part of any decision-making process:

Outcome analysis is looking at how a choice turned out.

Iterative learning is making changes to future choices based on what happened in the past.

The goal is to master results.

Informed choices give you control over what happens by:

Minimizing Bad Effects: Cutting down on unintended results.

Amplification of Desired Results: Making sure choices are in line with goals and objectives.

Conclusion

Informed decision-making is a mix of facts, feelings, beliefs, and technology that is always changing. By understanding and mastering this complicated dance, people and groups can make the way for the results they want, making their dreams come true.

Chapter 8: Practical Business Ideas:

Ancient Wisdom and AI-Enhanced Concepts

Timeless Business Concepts from the Past AI for Innovative Business Models

Crafting Ventures that Balance Tradition and Tech

Timeless Business Concepts from the Past

Introduction

In a business world where new models and strategies come out almost every day, it can be helpful to look back at timeless business ideas from ancient cultures. When mixed with AI- enhanced business practices from today, these historical gems offer entrepreneurs and business leaders a unique mix of wisdom and new ideas.

How important trust and a good name are

Ancient Wisdom: Trust and image have always been the most important parts of business, from ancient Mesopotamian traders to medieval European guilds. Without the laws and technology we have now, a person was only as good as their word and image.

AI with a modern twist: Today, trust and openness in transactions are made possible by AI- driven systems like blockchain and smart contracts. AI is used by online review sites to track and report customer feedback, which puts more emphasis on reputation.

"Trust but verify." — Russian saying

Diversification: Don't put all your eggs in one basket

Ancient wisdom: ancient dealers and merchants knew that putting all of their resources in one place was risky. They spread out their investments, trade routes, and goods.

AI adds a modern twist: Portfolio management algorithms and AI-powered market analysis tools help companies diversify their investments and operations by showing them where there are opportunities for growth and where there are risks.

The Fair Exchange Principle

Ancient Wisdom: The ancient Egyptians used the Ma'at principle, which stressed balance and justice. Fair exchange in trade and business was thought to be the key to keeping society in balance.

Modern twist with AI: Algorithms for price optimization make sure that prices are fair, and tools for the supply chain that are backed by AI make sure that quality is good. This furthers the idea of fair trade in modern business.

Customer-centeredness: putting the customer first

Ancient Wisdom: Bazaars and markets in the past did well by knowing their customers. From Roman market sellers to Chinese silk traders, it was very important to know what customers wanted and to give it to them.

1. Modern twist with AI: Modern Customer Relationship Management (CRM) systems use AI to better understand customer behaviors, preferences, and needs so they can give personalized experiences and solutions.

Learning and changing all the time Ancient Wisdom: From the universities of Timbuktu to the libraries of Alexandria, people have respected the idea of ongoing learning because it helps businesses change and grow.

AI adds a modern twist: Data analytics and market research tools powered by AI give companies constant insights that help them respond quickly to changes in the market.

Making friends and building networks

Ancient Wisdom: The famous Silk Road wasn't just about trade; it was also about building relationships and networks across different cultures and areas.

AI adds a modern twist: With AI-powered social media data and digital marketing platforms, businesses can build relationships and grow their networks on a global scale that has never been seen before.

Conclusion

Even though they come from a different time, many old business ideas are still very relevant in the business world today. Modern businesses can find a good mix between age-old wisdom and cutting-edge innovation by combining these timeless principles with tools and methods that are improved by AI.

AI for Developing New Business Model

Introduction

As companies try to adapt to the digital age, artificial intelligence (AI) is becoming a key driver of new ideas. AI has the ability to change business models themselves, in addition to automating tasks. This chapter shows how AI can be used to create new business models that give companies an edge in the fast-paced market of today.

1. Understand how AI can change things

At its core, AI is about handling data, recognizing patterns, and automating tasks. Its real transformative power comes from its ability to learn and change on its own, giving insights and efficiencies that can't be found anywhere else.

"In the future, business will be driven not just by data, but also by the insights that come from that data."

2. Customization on a large scale

Traditional Model: Businesses often have to choose between making their services more personalized and making their operations bigger.

AI-driven innovation: With AI, companies can give a large number of people very personalized experiences at the same time. Machine-learning algorithms look at each person's preferences to customize goods, services, and marketing messages. This makes customers feel like their needs are being met in a unique way.

3. Models for changing prices

Fixed prices or prices that change with the seasons.

AI-driven innovation: AI can look at a number of factors, like changes in demand and the prices of competitors, in real time and change prices on the fly to maximize profits and stay competitive in the market.

Subscriptions and Reordering Based on Past Behavior

Traditional Model: Sales that happen once.

AI-driven innovation: Businesses can switch to membership models or predictive reordering by using AI to study how customers use their products. This makes sure that products are always available when the customer needs them.

4. Making decisions in different places

Traditional Model: Key choices come from a small group or person at the center of the system.

AI-Driven Innovation: AI-driven data analytics can give different parts of a business real-time information, making it easier for everyone to make smart, decentralized decisions.

5. Service that goes above and beyond

Traditional Model: Customer service that is reactive, meaning that problems are dealt with after they happen.

AI-driven innovation: AI can predict where customers might have problems, so businesses can deal with problems before they get worse. This has a huge impact on customer happiness.

Innovation and product development with help from the crowd

Traditional Model: R&D teams in places where they can't be seen.

AI-Driven Innovation: Businesses can use customer feedback and new market trends in product development with the help of AI-driven sentiment analysis and trend forecasts. This makes innovation more open and crowdsourced.

6. Automation and how jobs are changing

Traditional Model: Operations jobs are done by hand.

AI-Driven Innovation: Automating repetitive tasks makes the business more efficient and frees up people to work on more important and creative parts of the business. This change changes the way organizations are set up and how jobs are done, putting a premium on creativity and working together with AI.

Conclusion

AI isn't just another tool in the business world; it's a force that changes everything. By looking at standard business models through the lens of AI, companies can come up with new ideas that were thought to be impossible before. The future of business belongs to those who can easily integrate AI's power into their core strategies, making innovation a daily standard instead of an occasional spark.

How to Make Businesses that Balance Tradition and Technology

Introduction

At the crossroads of time, where custom and the never-ending advance of technology meet, it's hard for businesses to find a way to combine the best of both worlds. The best business ideas are those that combine age-old wisdom with the latest technology advances in a way that works well. This part has some ideas about how to find this delicate balance.

1.   The Value of Business Traditions

Before we mix, let's look at why custom is important:

Building trust: Traditions often have a trust factor built in to them. They fit in well with the cultures and beliefs of the area.

Approaches that have been used for a long time: Traditional ways have often been improved over time.

"Tradition is not about keeping the ashes, but about passing on the light." —Georg Mahler

2.   Technology: The unstoppable force for change

The digital age has brought about a time of change:

Efficiency and size: Technology lets businesses operate on a size that has never been seen before.

Global Reach: Technology makes businesses global by getting rid of regional boundaries.

Adaptability: In markets that change quickly, technology gives us the tools we need to change quickly.

3. Tradition and technology working well together: examples

E-Commerce for Artisan Goods: Websites that sell handmade, traditional goods, bringing together traditional artistry and online markets.

Virtual Heritage Tours: Using VR and AR to give immersive experiences of historical places.

Digital Payment for Local Services: Adding tech solutions like mobile payments to traditional local services like local markets and rickshaw rides.

4. How to Know Which Traditions Are Worth Keeping

Not every old custom is useful in the current world. Companies have to: Check to see if the practice is still important to people today.

Analyze Efficiency: Is custom useful or is it just for feelings?

5. Making sure that technology fits with traditional beliefs

Cultural Sensitivity in AI is the process of teaching AI tools to respect and understand local customs and rules.

Keeping tradition in mind when designing tech: Digital platforms can use traditional aspects of design, aesthetics, and user experiences.

6. Problems with combining old and new tech

Obstacle to Change: Technology may be hard to integrate into traditional areas.

Over-digitization: Using technology too much can take away from the value of traditional services or goods.

7. Making a business model that works well together

To make a good blend:

Stakeholder education is teaching traditional craftspeople or workers about how technology can help them.

Approach that focuses on the customer: Make sure that the connection makes the customer's experience better.

Continuous Feedback Loop: Get feedback on a regular basis to improve and perfect the mix.

Conclusion

To find a good balance between custom and technology, you don't have to pick one over the other. Instead, you need to know what each is good at. In a world that values both authenticity and creativity more and more, businesses that combine tradition and technology well stand to make a lot of money and have a big impact on society.

Module 2:

Foundations of Abundance

Chapter 9: Budgeting with Ancient Wisdom and AI

Chapter 10: Ethical Investing: Balancing Ancient Virtues and AI

Chapter 11: Wealth Accumulation Strategies through Ages and Algorithms Chapter 12: Practical Money-Making Ventures for Families

Chapter 9: Budgeting with Ancient Wisdom and AI

Budgeting is an important business skill that has been around for a long time. Civilizations have done well for thousands of years by being careful about how they use their resources. At the heart of these old ways of doing things are ideals, traditions, and knowledge that have been passed down from generation to generation. But as our societies change and ideals of independence become more important, there is a chance that these important lessons will become less clear. In the age of technology, AI is a bridge that connects us to old knowledge and makes sure it stays around.

How ancient people made budgets?

In ancient times, making a budget was closely connected to family, community, and social values:

Family and community: Making a budget wasn't just something I did for myself. Families and groups worked together and shared resources, information, and plans. This method made sure that everyone grew and did well.

Financial knowledge was passed down from one generation to the next. It wasn't learned from books, but from real-life experiences. Elders were very important in making sure that younger members had the skills they needed to be financially stable.

Budgeting based on values: In the past, budgeting choices were based on more than just material needs. Spiritual, cultural, and community ideals were a big part of how resources were given out.

Modern Changes and What They Mean

Several changes have changed how we deal with spending in the modern world:

Independence Over Collective Wisdom: Putting a focus on individualism has its benefits, but it has also made it harder for many people to learn from their ancestors' collective wisdom.

Transient Knowledge: In today's fast-paced world, knowledge can become outdated quickly, and there isn't always a set way to pass on financial knowledge.

The Formal Education Gap: While schools prepare students for many parts of life, real financial education, especially budgeting, often takes a back seat.

AI is the link between the past and the present.

With its many skills, Artificial Intelligence can be a link between ancient wisdom and modern needs:

Knowledge preservation: AI can store, organize, and share old spending rules, making sure that everyone can use them.

Interactive Learning Platforms: Students can learn about budgeting in a way that fits with their culture and family practices through AI-powered platforms. This makes sure that the lessons stick with them.

Real-Time Budgeting Help: Modern AI tools can give feedback on budgeting choices in real time, based on ancient wisdom but adapted for modern problems.

Integrating budgeting into the curriculum: AI can help schools make lessons that combine old knowledge with new methods, giving students a well-rounded understanding of how to budget.

Conclusion

The core of planning, which is based on hundreds of years of shared knowledge, is too important to be lost to time or social changes. We are on the verge of a technology revolution, and AI is a lighthouse that makes sure the treasures of the past help us make decisions in the present. By combining old knowledge with AI, we can create a world where budgeting is not just a skill, but also a treasured legacy.

Ancient Budgeting Techniques

Old ways of making a budget

Our ancestors came up with amazing ways to use their resources well in many different countries and times. Even though they didn't have the tools we have today, they were able to use basic budgeting principles that were deeply connected to their way of life, values, and customs. These tried-and-true methods give you deep insights into the art of managing money.

The Envelope System: This is one of the oldest and easiest ways to budget. Families would put money for different costs into different envelopes. Each envelope had a theme on it, such as food, clothing, or celebrations. When the money in an envelope ran out, that area of spending stopped until the next budgeting period.

Before there was money, people used to trade. Each family would make a list of what they needed and then trade things or services to meet those needs. For this method to work, people had to think carefully about what they could give and what they needed in return, so that there was a balance of giving and getting.

The Granary Principle: In societies based on farming, the granary or storehouse was a key part of planning. After the harvest, grains were stored and given out in small amounts throughout the year to make sure there was enough food to last until the next crop.

Community pools: In many old cultures, people worked together to share resources. Each person would put some of what they earned or what they grew into a communal fund. This fund would then be used for group needs, situations, or community projects.

Keeping a ledger: Even though they were simple, many old cultures had their own ledgers, like tally sticks, clay tablets, or papyrus scrolls. These helped them keep track of their income, spending, bills, and credits, giving them a clear picture of their financial situation.

The idea behind zero-based budgeting was simple: every time you made a budget, you would start from zero. This made sure that people only spent money on what was really important by making them justify every expense.

Rotation savings: Sometimes called "chit funds" or "tandas" in some countries, this is when people put money into a communal pot on a regular basis. Every cycle, a different person takes the whole amount, so that everyone gets a lump sum at different times.

Lunar budgeting: From the Mayans to the Chinese, many old cultures used lunar dates. They made their budgets based on the phases of the moon, which often matched up with agricultural cycles, so that their money choices were in sync with the moon.

These methods, which are deeply rooted in their times, show how smart our ancestors were. Their ideas about discipline, helping each other, and making the most of what you have still apply today. In the modern world, going back to these old methods and putting them to use can give a new viewpoint and strengthen the basics of good money management.

Automating Budgeting with AI

In this age of automation, when machines and formulas control many parts of our lives, budgeting is no different. We are now in the middle of a paradigm shift. In the past, ledger books, abacuses, and hand math were the norm. With its incredible ability to solve problems, Artificial Intelligence offers a new way to handle money. But can a machine really understand all the details and complexities of how people spend their money? As we go through this chapter, we'll find out how AI is changing the world of budgeting in deep ways, making it not only more efficient but also a lot smarter.

Why Use a Budgeting Program?

Many people find it hard to make a budget. Keeping careful records of your income, spending, savings, and investments takes time, patience, and, often, a certain level of skill.

Efficiency: Automation makes sure that data is processed quickly and saves people from having to do tedious calculations by hand.

Accuracy: It's in our nature to make mistakes, especially when doing things over and over again. Once AI algorithms are set, these mistakes are taken care of, so planning is accurate.

Predictive Insights: AI doesn't just add up numbers; it also makes predictions. By looking at patterns, it can tell us a lot about the financial habits and trends of the future.

Putting AI and budgeting together

Data Aggregation: With so many bank accounts, investments, and ways to spend money, AI can easily combine data from many different sources to give a full picture of a person's funds.

Expense Categorization: By looking at the details of transactions, AI can automatically put costs into categories that help users see where their money goes.

Customized budgeting plans: Based on an individual's income, spending habits, and financial goals, AI can make customized budgeting plans that help people make the most of their money.

Real-time alerts: Whether you're getting close to your budget limit or there's an unusual transaction, AI makes sure you know right away. This helps you handle your money more proactively.

Investment Insights: Advanced AI tools look at market trends to make investment ideas that are in line with a person's financial goals and willingness to take risks.

Putting a human touch on budgeting software

AI offers accuracy and speed, but budgeting isn't just about numbers. Emotions, goals, and unplanned events in people's lives are very important.

Emotional intelligence in AI: The most advanced AI systems are made to understand how people feel and act. For example, if a person's spending goes up because of feelings, AI can spot this pattern and help or make suggestions.

Ethics: Because AI systems deal with sensitive financial data, it's important to make sure they follow strict ethics rules and put user privacy and data security first.

Conclusion

The goal of using AI to automate planning is not to get rid of the human touch, but to improve it. As these programs become a bigger part of our lives, they offer a mix of efficiency and personalization. This makes managing our money easier and more in line with our goals and dreams. When we use AI to make a budget, it's like having a wise financial advisor by our side who mixes the best of old wisdom and new technology.

Achieving Financial Harmony with Tradition and Tech

In a time when technology changes quickly and often threatens to make old ways of doing things obsolete, finding a balance is the key to making real progress. When we talk about money, this balance is even more important because it ties together the concrete threads of money with the intangible threads of ideals, traditions, and goals. This chapter digs deep into the ways that old financial practices and new technology tools work well together. It looks at the rich tapestry that is made when these two worlds come together.

How to get your finances in order

To understand financial balance, it's important to first know what makes it up:

Tradition: This is a summary of the values, beliefs, and habits that have been passed down from generation to generation, and it can help you make financial decisions.

Technology: Modern tools, especially AI-driven platforms, that make financial managing easier, better, and more efficient.

Walking on a Tightrope: Striking a Balance

Embracing Tradition: Our ancestors knew a lot about how to handle money because they were simple, wise, and thought ahead. By knowing and living by these rules, our financial journey will be based on wisdom.

Getting used to modern tools: AI and other financial technologies aren't just tools; they're also drivers. They let us use ancient knowledge in modern situations and come up with answers that fit the times.

Synergies in the Real World

Values-driven AI: Imagine an AI tool that doesn't just divide budgets based on numbers, but also takes into account your cultural and family values. These kinds of integrations make sure that technology doesn't replace custom but instead makes it more useful.

Tech-Enabled Financial Rituals: Rituals are a big part of many traditions. Adding tech tools to these traditions, like an AI-powered financial diary during the holidays or an algorithm that copies old ways of saving, brings them into the 21st century.

Analysis that looks at culture: AI tools of today can predict financial trends. But what if they also knew about traditional and culture events? This combination makes sure that you have enough money for a neighborhood event or a family milestone.

How to Keep People in a Digital World

As we move forward and use the many tech tools at our hands, it's important to remember that money is about people. At its core, money is about goals, protection, and leaving a legacy. AI gives us accuracy, analytics, and ways to improve, but tradition gives us perspective, ideals, and a sense of who we are. When you combine the two, your financial trip will be not only successful but also very meaningful.

Conclusion

Getting your finances in order requires an agreement between the old and the new, the traditional and the modern. It's about appreciating the knowledge of our ancestors and making it stronger with the tools we have now. We find a rich, rewarding, and deeply satisfying financial road plan in this delicate balance.

Chapter 10: Ethical Investing: Balancing Ancient Virtues and AI

Ancient Virtues in Investment Choices Ethical Investing Enhanced by AI 1 Prosperity through Ethical Commitments

Ancient Virtues in Investment Choices

In the long past of people, the idea of ethical investing isn't new, even if the words are new. In every culture, our ancestors knew it was important to make financial choices that were in line with larger moral, ethical, and social values. Their decisions were based on the values of society, sustainability, and long-term well-being. As we look at the core of ancient virtues and how they relate to investment choices, we find that they are very similar to the ethical investing models of today.

How Ancient Virtues Can Help You Invest.

Community-centeredness: In the past, the idea of "community" was the most important thing. Investments weren't just about individual gain; they were also about group prosperity. Investing in a local craftsman's business or backing new ideas in agriculture wasn't just a way to make money; it was also a promise to help the community.

Sustainability and Stewardship: Our ancestors knew that resources were limited and needed to be taken care of. Investments were often made in things that would last, whether it was in terms of resources, society, or skills. The goal was to leave the next generation a world that was at least as good as their own.

Integrity and openness: In the past, trade, barter, and money trades were based on trust. Honesty was a highly valued trait, and investments in businesses that were open and honest were highly valued.

How to Understand Ancient Virtues in a Modern World

Social Responsibility: Just as people in the past put the well-being of their communities first, social responsibility is a big part of ethical investment today. With old knowledge in hand, modern investors tend to back businesses that put people before profits.

Taking the environment into account: Ethical investors today value eco-friendly businesses because their ancestors taught them to respect nature and resources and because they know that true wealth also means leaving the next generation a healthier world.

Ethical Business Practices: Being honest, open, and doing the right thing are ancient values that are still important today. Ethical investors today support companies that are open about how they do business, are fair to their employees, and act with moral integrity.

The Effects of Making Good Moral Decisions

Our ancestors knew that investments are a good way to make money. They aren't just about money; they can also lead to big changes. By putting money into projects that are based on ethics, donors set off a chain reaction. These investments help companies that do good things for society. This creates a cycle of good.

Conclusion

A common saying says, "What's past is prologue." Ancient virtues that influenced business decisions can teach investors of today a lot. They remind us that investing isn't just about getting money back; it's also about leaving a good legacy. When we combine these time-tested principles with modern business tools and data analysis, we create a financial landscape that is not only prosperous but also based on strong values.

Ancient Virtues in Investment Choices

Due to technology and the changing needs of modern society, the world moves at a speed that has never been seen before. This makes it hard for investors to make choices that are morally sound in such a fast-paced environment. With its ability to analyze data, make predictions, and change, Artificial Intelligence (AI) provides chances to improve ethical investments that have never been seen before. Let's learn more about how AI is changing the way people make socially sound financial decisions.

AI: The New Guide to Ethical Investments

Unbiased Analysis: One of AI's best features is that it can process huge amounts of data without favoring one thing over another. By looking at how businesses work, their financial histories, and how they affect the environment, AI can give investors unbiased information about how ethically sound different investment options are.

Analysis of Long-Term Effects: AI can predict the long-term effects of investment choices by figuring out how they might affect the environment and society. This ability to predict the future lets investors look at not only the short-term returns, but also the long-term ethical effects of their decisions.

Ethical standards can be changed. No two investors have the same moral sense. AI-driven platforms can be changed to fit each person's values, sifting through investment chances and suggesting ones that make sense with those values.

Bringing together old values and AI skills

Data-Driven Community Impact: Using the ancient virtue of caring about the community, AI reviews how investments might affect the community, making sure that money goes to projects that help people.

Sustainability Metrics: Following in the footsteps of our ancestors' respect for sustainability, AI programs can measure a company's ecological footprint. This makes sure that investments go to businesses that are good for the environment.

Transparency and Accountability: Using AI, investors can keep an eye on how businesses act ethically in real time. This way, they can make sure that their investments stay in line with the age-old values of honesty and openness.

What's going on and how to move forward.

AI gives powerful tools for responsible investing, but it's important to know its limits:

Accuracy of Data: AI can only make suggestions as good as the data it is given. For truly ethical results, it's important to make sure the data is correct and fair.

Too much dependence on technology: Artificial intelligence (AI) is a helpful tool, but human judgment based on ancient knowledge is still unbeatable. The key is to find a mix between AI's suggestions and human judgment.

Conclusion

AI is, at its core, a tool—a very powerful one—that can change the way ethical investment works. By combining the deep morals of our ancestors with the analytical skills of AI, investors can manage the modern financial maze with a compass that is both technologically advanced and morally grounded. When tradition and technology work together like this, the future of ethical investment looks bright and hopeful.

Prosperity through Ethical Commitments

Since the beginning of time, people have always wanted to be rich. But what does real wealth mean? Is it just about getting rich, or does it have a deeper, more complete meaning? When we combine what we know about wealth today with what we know about it in the past, we find an important truth: true prosperity is tied to moral values. Let's figure out how ethics and wealth go hand in hand with each other.

What Does Ethical Prosperity Mean?

True wealth isn't just about how much money someone has or what they own. Instead, it's a wide-ranging idea that includes:

Financial stability means having enough money to meet your basic needs and live in comfort.

The health, happiness, and mental well-being of oneself, one's family, and the community as a whole.

Positive Legacy: Leaving the world and future generations with something good that will last. The part that moral commitments play in making people successful

Building Trust and Reputation: Ethical promises, especially when it comes to money, help stakeholders trust each other. Over time, this trust leads to a strong image, which can lead to bigger opportunities and partnerships.

Making sure of long-term success: Ethical investments are often in line with responsible and healthy practices, which makes sure of their longevity. Businesses that are run in an ethical way can handle social and economic changes better and are better set up for long-term success.

Ethical obligations are in line with a person's core values, which makes them more fulfilling. When money choices are in line with personal values, it makes people feel happier and more at peace.

Fostering Community Development: Community well-being and prosperity go hand in hand. By putting money and time into improving the community, one creates a place where everyone can thrive and feel safe.

Applications for Today: Putting Ethical Commitments into Action

Businesses that put their ethical responsibilities first today see real benefits. As an example:

Consumer believe: People believe and stay loyal to brands that are open, fair, and responsible.

Satisfaction of Employees: Ethical obligations boost morale, which leads to more work and less turnover.

Environmental and Social Returns: Businesses that care about the environment and how they affect society often benefit from both a healthier world and a community that cares about them.

Conclusion

The way to real prosperity goes through the areas of ethics, integrity, and responsibility. It tells us that pursuing wealth with a good heart not only makes us better off financially, but also spiritually and emotionally. As we stand at the intersection of ancient virtues and modern possibilities, we realize that an old saying is true: the ethical road is always the most rewarding, even when it's hard. By following moral rules, we plant the seeds for a good future, not just for ourselves but for future generations as well.

Chapter 11: Wealth Accumulation Strategies through Ages and Algorithms

Lessons from Ancient Wealth Accumulation AI-Driven Wealth Accumulation Techniques

Fusing Past and Future for Financial Abundance

Lessons from Ancient Wealth Accumulation

People have been looking for ways to get rich and protect their financial futures since the beginning of time. By looking at how ancient societies built up their wealth, we can learn valuable lessons that are still useful in the age of algorithms and modern financial systems. This chapter looks at what we can learn from how our ancestors lived and how we can use those lessons to build wealth today.

1. Trading and Bartering:

In the past, people usually got rich from things they could touch, like food, animals, and goods. The barter system made it easy for these goods to be traded, and it was the basis for economic interactions. Even though modern economies are based on money, the idea of trading value for value hasn't changed. Algorithmic trading platforms and decentralized finance (DeFi) can be thought of as current versions of the barter system because they allow automated exchanges to happen without a middleman.

2. Farming and Property Rights:

Agriculture was the main way that people in early civilizations made money. When people and groups owned rich land, they could grow food and other things they needed. Investing in real estate is still a great way to build wealth today. Algorithms help investors figure out what to do by studying property values, rental incomes, and market trends.

3. Valuable metals and other goods:

Ancient people valued gold and silver because they were hard to find and would last for a long time. These metals were used as money and as ways to store wealth. In the same way, modernbuyers use commodities like gold as a way to protect themselves from economic risk. Algorithms are now used to buy and sell goods in the best way possible in split-second intervals.

4. Getting Knowledge and Skills:

In the past, getting specialized information or skills was often the way to get rich. Blacksmiths, writers, and traders all had skills that made them stand out. Education is still a way to get ahead in life. Algorithms have changed the way people can get an education by making online learning and individualized skill development possible.

5. Exchange of ideas and networks:

Ancient trade lines made it easier for people from different cultures to meet and for goods to move from one place to another. Today's globalized economy lives on how well everything is linked together. Algorithms and networking platforms on social media make it easier to meet new people and grow your impact.

6. Time and the effect of compounding:

Getting rich in the past took time. Over the years, crops grew, herds grew, and investments grew older. This basic idea hasn't changed. The power of compounding, which is increased by algorithms that automatically add to investments and rebalance portfolios, shows how important it is to be patient when trying to build up a lot of wealth

7. Taking care of risks and spreading them out:

Traders in the past sent their goods on many different ways to reduce the risk of theft or loss. Diversifying investments is still a key part of current financial planning. Advanced algorithms look at risk factors, which lets buyers make diversified portfolios and reduce the chance of losing money.

8.   Leaving a legacy and passing on wealth:

In ancient times, it was very important for wealth to be passed down from one family to the next. Today, estate planning and investment algorithms help keep and grow wealth from one family to the next, making sure that it lasts.

Conclusion

The ways that ancient civilizations made money are based on timeless principles that are very similar to the way that algorithms drive current financial practices. By accepting the lessons of history and adapting them to the digital age, people can find their way through the complicated process of building wealth and secure their financial futures in a world that is always changing.

AI-Driven Wealth Accumulation Techniques

Introduction

In the digital age, the use of artificial intelligence (AI) has changed the way that people try to get rich. AI's ability to handle huge amounts of data, find patterns, and make choices based on data has changed how people and institutions build and manage their wealth. This chapter goes into detail about the new ways to make money that are being made possible by AI.

1.   Trading by computer:

AI-driven algorithmic trade has become a key way for people to get rich in the modern world. These algorithms work very quickly and accurately to analyze market data, make trades, and handle portfolios. Machine learning algorithms can adapt to market changes and learn from them. This lets traders take advantage of chances that might not be obvious to a human analyst.

2. Investment Predictive Analytics:

AI-driven predictive analytics give information about possible market trends. Machine learning models look at past data, market signs, and even news and social media to figure out how an investment will turn out. This helps investors make well-informed choices and change their plans as needed.

3. Automated advisors:

Robo-advisors are platforms that use artificial intelligence to give personalized investment advice and handle portfolios. Robo-advisors make and handle portfolios that are best for growth by looking at a person's risk tolerance, financial goals, and market conditions. This technology makes wealth management more democratic by making it possible for more people to use.

4. Risk management and the search for fraud:

AI programs are good at finding strange patterns and outliers in financial activities. This ability is important for catching fraud and managing risks, which keeps investments and financial activities safe.

5. Planning for your own money:

AI looks at a person's finances, goals, and willingness to take risks to make personalized financial plans. These plans help people reach their goals of building wealth by giving them step-by-step advice on things like planning, paying down debt, and making investments.

6. Analysis of how people feel and market trends:

AI looks at news stories, social media posts, and other online sources to figure out how people feel about certain stocks or markets. This research can give you important information about how the market might change and how investors might act.

7. Tips for Investing in Real Estate:

AI algorithms handle data on property values, rental incomes, neighborhood trends, and even local economic indicators to help investors make smart choices about real estate investments.

8. Learning and changing all the time:

One of the best things about AI is that it can learn and change. AI systems get better over time as they learn from more data and experiences and improve their methods and decision-making processes.

Conclusion

When AI-driven techniques are added to methods for building wealth, it opens up a whole new world of possibilities. AI algorithms are helpful in handling the complex modern financial markets because they are fast, accurate, and based on data. As more and more people and organizations use these technologies, the path to getting rich gets smarter, faster, and easier for a wider range of people to take. But it's important to remember that AI can help people make better decisions, but it should be used with human judgment and control for the best results.

Fusing Past and Future for Financial Abundance

As we stand at the crossroads of history and technology, the key to making a lot of money is to combine the timeless knowledge of the past with the cutting-edge technology of the future.

This chapter looks at how old ideas and new technologies can be used together in a way that works well. It offers a holistic way to build wealth that can be used by people of all ages.

Taking Time-Tested Principles to Heart:

Ancient strategies for building wealth, such as diversification, patience, and managing risks wisely, give us a strong basis for success. These ideas have stood the test of time and can be easily combined with new technologies to help you manage the complicated financial world of today.

Using AI to Make Informed Decisions: The rise of AI has made it possible to get insights from data that weren't possible before. By using AI's analytical skills, people can make smart investment choices based on historical data, market trends, and predictive analytics, which increases their chances of growing their money.

Long-Term Thinking and Compounding: The idea of compounding has its roots in ancient farming techniques, and it works well with algorithms that are driven by AI. Algorithms can automate regular investments and make sure portfolios are set up for long-term growth. This works well with the time-tested concept of letting money grow slowly over time.

Personalization and customization: Just as old craftsmen changed their work to fit the needs of each customer, AI-driven platforms today offer customized financial strategies. These systems look at a person's goals, willingness to take risks, and current financial situation to make personalized investment plans. This makes building wealth easier and more effective.

Cultural Wisdom and Global Connectivity: In the past, people from different countries got along well and shared ideas. Today, global investment possibilities and instant communication are made possible by digital platforms and algorithms. People can access a wider range of investments and relationships if they learn from different cultures and use modern technology.

Legacy planning and intergenerational wealth: Using both old ways of keeping wealth in the family and new tools for estate planning that are driven by AI makes sure that wealth is passed on smoothly to the next generation. Intelligent algorithms help people manage their assets, taxes, and legal issues, which protects their estate.

Finding a balance between human intuition and the precision of technology. AI is great at handling and analyzing data, but human intuition and judgment are still very important. When humans and AI work together, they create a synergy that helps people manage the ever-changing financial world with caution and flexibility.

Financial Abundance: The goal of having financial abundance isn't just to get rich. It's also to live a balanced and satisfying life. By adopting practices from ancient philosophies that emphasize being present and happy, people can develop a good relationship with gaining wealth, which is important for achieving overall prosperity.

When ancient wisdom and current technology are used together to make money, it gives a complete plan for getting rich. By learning from the past and using AI and algorithms to their full potential, people can create a road to prosperity that respects tradition, embraces innovation, and creates a bright future for themselves and future generations.

Chapter 12: Practical Money-Making Ventures for Families

Family-Friendly Money-Making Opportunities AI-Powered Side Hustles for Income

Fostering Family Entrepreneurship for Growth

Family-Friendly Money-Making Opportunities

In today's fast-paced world, more and more families are looking for ways to make more money while keeping a good work-life balance. There are a lot of ways to make money that are good for the whole family. This means that families can make extra money while spending important time together. This chapter looks at several useful things that families can do to improve their financial situation.

Online e-commerce businesses: The rise of online marketplaces has made it possible for families to start e-commerce companies from the comfort of their own homes. Families can use their creativity and entrepreneurial energy while making their own schedules by selling handmade crafts, vintage items, or unique goods.

Tutoring and Educational Services: Families with members who are good at languages, music, or academic subjects can give tutoring or educational services. This not only brings in money, but it also helps the family and their group learn.

Home-based baking and cooking: If your family is good at cooking, you could start a home- based baking business or a catering business. Making special cakes, cookies, or meals for events can be a creative way to make money and use your skills.

Pet sitting and pet care: Families who love animals can have fun and make money by giving services like pet sitting, dog walking, and pet grooming. This business lets family members spend time with pets and make money at the same time.

Gardening and landscaping services: Families with green thumbs can help their neighbors and local companies with gardening and landscaping. This outdoor business not only brings in money, but it also adds to the beauty of the area.

Planning and hosting events: Events, parties, and classes can be put together by the whole family. Using the hobbies and skills of different family members makes it possible to plan and host events in a well-rounded way.

Making content and blogging: Families who like to write, take pictures, or make videos can start a blog or YouTube page. Sharing ideas, experiences, or skills online can bring in an audience, which could lead to money from ads and donations.

Home Improvement and Do-It-Yourself Services: Families who know how to fix up their homes can offer services like painting, carpentry, and interior design. This business not only makes money, but it also makes homes and living areas better.

Fitness and wellness coaching: Families who care a lot about health and wellness can find it rewarding to work as fitness trainers or wellness teachers. You can make money and help people feel better by leading group workouts, giving nutritional tips, or holding mindfulness sessions.

Virtual Assistance and Administrative Services: Families with good organizational and administrative skills can help companies and individuals with their work online. Tasks like organizing, bookkeeping, and managing social media can be done from afar.

Family-friendly ways to make money allow families to not only add to their incomes but also share important experiences and strengthen their bonds with each other. Families can start their own businesses that make money and give them the chance to spend time together. They can do this by finding ventures that fit with their hobbies, skills, and values.

AI-Powered Side Hustles for Income

Introduction:

The incorporation of artificial intelligence (AI) into numerous businesses has paved the way for novel side hustle that take advantage of cutting-edge technology. These AI-powered companies allow individuals to earn extra money while leveraging the powers of automation, data analysis, and machine learning. This chapter looks at a variety of AI-powered side hustle that can help you make money.

1. **Chatbot Development:** A lucrative side hustle is creating and selling AI-powered chatbots to organizations for customer care or sales interactions. As AI algorithms progress, so does the desire for personalized, automated client experiences.

2. **Data Analysis and Insights:** Data analysts can provide services to small firms looking to gain insights from their data. AI algorithms aid in the processing of massive datasets and the generation of useful insights that inform business decisions.

3. **Content Generation and Copywriting:** AI-powered content generators help with blog entries, social media content, and product descriptions. Freelancers can use this technology to efficiently offer high-quality written content.

4. **Social Media Management:** AI systems can monitor social media trends and engagement patterns, assisting individuals in managing and optimizing business social media accounts. Curating material, scheduling postings, and tracking metrics are all part of this side hustle.

5. **Stock Trading Algorithms:** Those with a knack for finance and programming might make a fortune designing AI-powered stock

trading algorithms. These algorithms use machine learning to assess market data and execute trades with little human interaction.

6. **Language Translation Services:** While AI-powered language translation systems have advanced tremendously, human touch remains critical for accuracy and context. Offering translation and localization services in addition to AI tools can provide you a competitive advantage.

7. **Image and video editing:** AI-powered image and video editing tools make the editing process more accessible and efficient for creative side hustlers. Offering photo retouching or video montage making services might be beneficial.

8. **Personal Finance Advising:** Using AI-powered financial planning tools, individuals can provide tailored financial advice to others in order to help them manage their budgets, investments, and debt. Clients benefit from the combination of human experience and AI insights.

9. **Health and Fitness Coaching:** AI-powered fitness apps can log exercises, make nutrition recommendations, and track progress. Fitness side hustlers can assist consumers via customised training and wellness programs that include AI-generated advice.

10. **E-commerce Optimization:** Entrepreneurs can provide online firms with AI-driven e- commerce optimization services. AI algorithms monitor customer behavior, recommend items, and improve user experiences, resulting in increased conversions.

Conclusion: AI-powered side hustles combine individual abilities with cutting-edge technology to provide a fresh approach to making cash. As AI capabilities evolve, innovative individuals can seize these possibilities to add value to businesses and consumers by using the power of automation and data analysis. Individuals can carve themselves distinct niches in the gig economy while contributing to their financial progress by embracing the promise of AI.

Fostering Family Entrepreneurship for Growth

Introduction: The notion of family entrepreneurship combines the dynamics of business with the power of familial relationships, producing a one-of-a-kind path to growth and success. This chapter looks into the concepts and practices that support family entrepreneurship, providing insights into how families can work together to collaborate, develop, and prosper in the commercial world.

Shared Vision and Values: A shared vision and set of values is at the heart of successful family entrepreneurship. Families should clarify their collective goals and match their aspirations with the company's vision, laying a solid basis for future success.

Leveraging Individual Strengths: Each family member brings a distinct set of skills to the table. Family companies can designate roles that enhance efficiency and productivity by identifying and leveraging each member's capabilities.

Open Communication: It is critical to avoid disagreements and guarantee that everyone is on the same page. Regular family meetings, open dialogue, and attentive listening assist to avoid misunderstandings and create unity.

Adaptability and Innovation: Family enterprises must adapt to shifting market trends and technologies. Long-term sustainability and competitiveness are ensured by encouraging an inventive mentality and being open to adaptation.

A Well-Defined Governance Structure: To avoid conflicts and power struggles, clearly defined roles, duties, and decision-making processes are vital. Creating a transparent governance framework aid in the maintenance of harmony and accountability.

Professionalism and Boundaries: It is critical to balance familial relationships with professionalism. Setting clear boundaries between personal and business matters aids in the maintenance of a good work environment and the reduction of conflicts.

Mentorship and Learning: Fostering a culture of continual learning and mentorship inside the family business enables skill development and knowledge sharing across generations.

Succession Planning: Future planning is essential in family businesses. A well-thought-out succession plan guarantees that leadership and responsibilities are passed on to the next generation smoothly.

Value Diversity: Diverse points of view help to innovation and well-rounded decision-making. In-laws or non-family members can bring new ideas and perspectives to the business.

Giving Back to the Community: Family businesses can make significant contributions to their communities. Participating in philanthropy, sustainability programs, or local relationships improves a company's brand and impact.

Maintaining a Work-Life Balance: Maintaining a work-life balance is critical for the well- being of both the business and the family. Setting limits and spending valuable family time helps to enhance relationships.

Honoring Achievements: Recognizing and honoring personal and professional milestones develops a sense of accomplishment and unity within the family.

Fostering family entrepreneurship is a journey that involves dedication, communication, and collaboration. Families can develop successful enterprises that not only contribute to their financial progress but also deepen family ties and leave a legacy for future generations by aligning shared values, using individual strengths, and embracing innovation.

Module 3:

Financial Health and Well-being Chapter 13: Emotional Intelligence in Finance

Chapter 14: Financial Stress and Mindful Practices

Chapter 15: Integrating Ancient Financial Wisdom with AI

Chapter 16: Ancient Savings Practices and Modern Technology:

Chapter 17: Legacy and Estate Planning

Chapter 18: Financial Education and Continuous Learning

Chapter 19: Wealth and Spiritual Growth

Chapter 13: Emotional Intelligence in Finance

Introduction:

Emotional intelligence (EI) plays a critical role in financial health and well-being that goes beyond numbers and computations. Understanding and controlling our own and others' emotions can have a significant impact on our financial decisions, relationships, and general well-being. This chapter examines the role of emotional intelligence in finance and how it contributes to making educated and balanced financial decisions.

1. **Define Emotional Intelligence:** Emotional intelligence is the ability to identify, comprehend, manage, and effectively use one's own and others' emotions. Self-awareness, self-regulation, empathy, and interpersonal skills are all required. These characteristics are very important in financial problems.

2. **Emotional Intelligence in Financial Decision**-Making: Emotions frequently influence our financial decisions, sometimes leading to irrational choices or behaviors. Developing emotional intelligence enables people to detect and regulate emotions that may cloud their judgment, allowing them to make decisions that are in line with their long-term goals.

3. **Self-Awareness and Money Mindset:** An important element of emotional intelligence is understanding one's emotions and underlying views regarding money. A healthy money attitude promotes a pleasant connection with money and improves spending, saving, and investing decisions.

4. **Self-Regulation and Impulse Control:** Emotionally intelligent

people are better able to handle impulsive spending or investing decisions that are motivated by fear or enthusiasm. Developing self-control abilities allows for more careful and rational financial decisions.

5. **Empathy and Interpersonal Relationships:** Empathy, a crucial component of emotional intelligence, helps to improve communication in financial relationships, whether with a spouse, family member, or financial advisor. Understanding the viewpoints and requirements of others can lead to mutually productive financial decisions.

6. **Dealing with Financial Stress and worry:** Emotional intelligence can help you deal with financial stress and worry. Individuals with higher EI can identify stress causes, create coping techniques, and seek help when necessary, resulting in improved emotional and financial well- being.

7. **Emotionally Intelligent Financial Communication:** When addressing financial concerns with family members or partners, emotional intelligent communication is vital. Conversations that are open, compassionate, and nonjudgmental promote understanding and collaboration.

8. **Resilience in the Face of Adversity:** Most people face financial adversity. Emotional intelligence promotes resilience, allowing people to recover from losses, learn from mistakes, and adjust their strategy.

9. Developing Emotional Intelligence: Emotional intelligence is developed via self-reflection, mindfulness, and practice. Journaling, meditation, and seeking professional counseling are all activities that can help with EI development.

10. **Balancing Emotional and Logical Decision-Making:** The necessity of logical and analytical decision-making is not diminished by emotional intelligence. Rather, it supplements rationality by treating emotions as valuable data points in decision-making.

Conclusion: Emotional intelligence can help you achieve financial health and well-being. Individuals can make informed financial decisions that match with their goals while maintaining strong relationships and overall emotional well-being by integrating self-awareness, self- regulation, empathy, and effective communication. A holistic approach to financial management is ensured by striking a balance between emotional and intellectual factors.

Ancient Origins of Emotional Intelligence Introduction:

Emotional intelligence (EI) is frequently related with modern psychology and human development. However, the origins of EI can be found in ancient cultures and philosophies that valued self-awareness, empathy, and emotional understanding. This chapter looks at how ancient wisdom and practices laid the groundwork for emotional intelligence development and its significance in today's environment.

1. **Ancient Philosophical Traditions:** Self-knowledge and self-mastery were highly valued by ancient civilizations such as the Greeks, Romans, and Eastern cultures. Philosophers such as Socrates, Confucius, and Aristotle emphasized the importance of understanding one's emotions and developing virtues such as patience, compassion, and equanimity.

2. **Mindfulness and Meditation techniques:** Mindfulness and meditation techniques established in ancient traditions such as Buddhism and Stoicism taught people to observe their thoughts and feelings without judgment. These techniques improved self-awareness, emotional management, and comprehension of the human psyche.

3. **Compassion and Empathy:** Compassion and empathy for others were frequently emphasized in ancient religious and spiritual teachings. In Hinduism, concepts such as "ahimsa" (nonviolence) and "agape" (unconditional love) in Christianity represent the awareness of emotions as essential to human connections.

4. **Mythology and Emotional Archetypes:** Ancient myths and stories frequently depicted complicated emotional experiences and archetypes to which people could relate. These stories provided insights into human behavior, emotions, and the difficulties associated with managing them.

5. **Rituals of Passage and Emotional Development:** Many ancient civilizations had rituals or rites of passage that marked the shift from one stage of life to another. These rituals, which frequently included emotional challenges, were intended to promote emotional growth, resilience, and a deeper awareness of oneself.

6. **Communication and Storytelling:** In ancient communities, effective communication was critical, and it was often accomplished through storytelling, art, and rituals. Individuals were able to connect emotionally, exchange experiences, and transfer cultural values through these modes of expression.

7. **Emotional Intelligence in Leadership:** In ancient times, leaders were expected to have emotional self-control, empathy, and the ability to inspire and guide others. These ideals were mirrored in the wisdom of kings such as Ashoka the Great of India and Marcus Aurelius of Rome.

8. **Integration into Modern activities:** ancient traditions' notions of emotional intelligence have found resonance in modern psychology and self-help activities. Mindfulness, empathy, and self-reflection are examples of concepts that have been reinterpreted and integrated into modern methods to personal growth.

Studying the emotional intelligence hidden in ancient wisdom can provide useful insights towards fostering emotional well-being and successful relationships. The time-tested strategies can provide direction in managing today's complex emotional landscape.

Conclusion: The wisdom of ancient civilizations has deep origins in emotional intelligence. Individuals can broaden their understanding of emotions, improve interpersonal connections, and develop emotional well-being in a way that resonates across time and cultures by accepting and embracing the lessons from various civilizations.

AI-Enhanced Financial and Emotional Awareness

Introduction: The combination of artificial intelligence (AI) and emotional awareness is changing how people perceive and regulate their emotions in the context of money. AI technologies provide individuals with tools and insights that can help them build a deeper knowledge of their financial emotions, allowing for better decision-making and emotional well-being. This chapter investigates the use of AI to improve emotional awareness in the field of personal finance.

1. **The Role of Emotions in Financial Decision-Making:** Emotions have a considerable influence on financial decisions, frequently leading to irrational choices or behavior. Understanding the emotional factors that drive financial decisions is critical for improving financial outcomes.

2. **AI's Analytical Capability:** AI technology can process massive volumes of data and detect patterns that humans may miss. AI can assist users in identifying relationships between emotional states and financial habits by leveraging this analytical capability.

3. **Sentiment Analysis in Financial Data:** Using news, social media, and market data, AI-driven sentiment analysis can determine public sentiment. This data sheds light on how emotional tendencies affect financial markets and investor behavior.

4. **Tracking Emotional Reactions to Financial Events:** AI-powered applications can track people's emotional reactions to financial events like market swings or investment results. This immediate response improves emotional self-awareness.

5. individualized Financial Coaching: AI-powered financial coaching services analyze users' financial behaviors and emotions to deliver individualized advice and solutions for reaching financial objectives.

6. Recognizing Biases and Emotional Triggers: AI can assist people in recognizing cognitive biases and emotional triggers that influence financial decisions. This awareness enables people to make more reasoned decisions and avoid impulsive behavior.

7. Emotional Stress Early Warning Systems: AI may detect indicators of emotional stress based on communication patterns and behavioral changes, warning users to the possible negative emotional consequences of financial actions.

8. AI-Assisted Budgeting and Spending Analysis: AI-powered budgeting systems may evaluate spending habits and offer adjustments that correspond with people' financial goals, reducing financial stress.

9. Integrating Emotional Well-being measures: Future AI applications could include emotional well-being measures with standard financial metrics, providing a more comprehensive picture of an individual's financial health

10. Ethical Considerations: As AI acquires access to deeply intimate emotional data, it is critical to ensure ethical use, data privacy, and informed consent.

Conclusion: The incorporation of AI-enhanced emotional awareness in personal finance represents a paradigm shift in how people approach financial decision-making. Individuals can make more informed, balanced, and emotionally intelligent financial decisions by harnessing AI's analytical ability to understand emotional patterns and triggers. This convergence of technology and emotional awareness has the potential to improve financial well-being and lead to a more positive relationship with money.

Chapter 14: Financial Stress and Mindful Practices

Achieving Financial Peace through Mindfulness

Age-Old Remedies for Financial Concerns

Financial stress is a typical component of modern living, affecting both mental and emotional well-being. Throughout history, societies all throughout the world have evolved wisdom and rituals to deal with the emotional toll that financial anxieties can take. This chapter delves at ancient cures from diverse traditions that can help you manage financial stress with mindfulness and resilience.

Stoicism and Detachment: Stoicism, which originated in ancient Greece, promotes emotional detachment from external conditions. Applying Stoic ideas helps people focus on what they can control, which reduces worry and promotes resilience in the face of financial difficulties.

Buddhist Impermanence Concepts: Buddhist teachings emphasize impermanence and the fleeting nature of earthly prosperity. Individuals can acquire a healthier perspective on financial problems by embracing impermanence, realizing that circumstances change, and finding calm during uncertainty.

Taoist Nature Harmony: Taoist philosophy promotes harmony with nature and the flow of life. Using Taoist concepts allows people to adapt and achieve balance in the face of financial hardships, generating a sense of calm.

Indigenous Community Values: Many indigenous cultures place a high value on community solidarity and resource sharing. Individuals can seek social connections, share their difficulties, and rely on their communities for emotional and practical support by drawing on these ideals.

Ancient Mindfulness techniques: Meditation, deep breathing, and yoga were ancient mindfulness techniques used across cultures to promote inner calm and resilience. These routines aid in stress management and emotional well-being.

Rituals and Ceremonies: Ancient rituals and ceremonies were frequently used to express and release emotions. Individuals might process financial issues by incorporating personal routines such as writing or gratitude practices.

Connecting with Nature: Ancient cultures had strong bonds with nature. Spending time in nature, forest bathing, or simply anchoring oneself outside can give peace and ease financial stress.

Expressive Arts Therapy: For generations, artistic expression has been utilized to resolve emotions. Painting, music, and dancing, for example, can serve as cathartic outlets for financial problems.

Developing thankfulness and Contentment: Ancient traditions frequently emphasized thankfulness and contentment as paths to inner calm. Individuals might reduce their concern about material needs by establishing gratitude for what they have and finding satisfaction in simplicity.

Integrating old Wisdom with current Practices: Integrating old remedies into current practices can improve their efficacy. Integrating mindfulness skills, gratitude practices, and emotional awareness with one's financial strategy can provide a comprehensive approach to financial stress management.

Conclusion: Ancient traditions can teach us how to deal with money issues with mindfulness and resilience. Individuals can negotiate present financial issues with a balanced perspective by drawing on the wisdom of the past, cultivating emotional well-being and enhancing their capacity to endure financial stress.

Achieving Financial Peace Through Mindfulness

Introduction:

Welcome to the transforming arena of gaining financial peace through mindfulness meditation. Finding a condition of serenity and equilibrium in the midst of financial concerns may appear to be a faraway objective. But don't worry; the ancient technique of mindfulness can help you navigate financial issues with grace and cultivate a sense of calm. Follow these steps to begin your road toward financial well-being and inner serenity.

1. **Embrace Mindfulness's Essence:** Begin by engaging yourself in the essence of mindfulness. Accept the concept of being present in the moment, without judgment. Allow your focus to be on your money difficulties without the weight of previous regrets or future concerns.

2. **Let Go of anxieties:** Let go of the money anxieties that cloud your mind. Practice acknowledging these concerns without overemphasizing them. Let go of the desire to obsess over previous financial blunders or future concerns.

3. **Pay Attention to Your Emotional Triggers:** As you progress, begin to pay attention to the emotional triggers that drive your financial habits. Recognize the emotions that occur in reaction to financial issues. Allow yourself to answer thoughtfully instead than impulsively.

4. **Foster a Healthy Money connection:** Shift your focus to creating a healthier money connection. Examine your financial attitudes, beliefs, and emotions with care. Allow your increased self-awareness to lead you to more balanced financial interactions.

5. **Beliefs and Intentions:** Get to the heart of your financial decisions by aligning them with your beliefs and priorities. Allow these ideas to guide you away from impulsive spending and toward thoughtful spending and saving.

6. **Accept Impermanence and Change:** Accept the wisdom of impermanence. Recognize that financial situations, like life itself, are constantly changing. Approach financial volatility with tenacity and openness.

7. **Tame Financial Stress:** Arm yourself with mindfulness methods like meditation and deep breathing to alleviate the physiological stress responses that financial worries can cause. Regular practice improves emotional well-being and protects you from the harmful effects of financial stress.

8. **Improve Decision-Making Skills:** Mindfulness can help you improve your decision-making skills. Make financial decisions with clarity and focus. Allow mindfulness to guide you to sensible and advantageous judgments.

9. **Accept thankfulness and Abundance:** Accept the current moment and nurture thankfulness for the resources available. Scarcity feelings fade when you adopt an abundant mindset, creating way for financial contentment.

10. **Practice Mindful Spending and Saving:** Practice mindful spending and saving to empower your financial decisions. Pause before making a purchase to consider its meaning. This technique helps you to match your behaviors with your long-term objectives.

11. **Practice Mindful Financial Planning:** Make time to practice mindful financial planning. Intentionally evaluate your goals, finances, and investments. Allow this exercise to instill clarity and purpose in your decisions.

Conclusion: You are now ready to go on a journey toward financial peace through mindfulness. By incorporating mindfulness into your financial practices, you will be able to negotiate problems with grace, foster emotional well-being, and find contentment in your financial journey. Remember that each stage is a gateway to a peaceful relationship with your finances and, ultimately, with yourself as you follow these directions.

Chapter 15: Integrating Ancient Financial Wisdom with AI

Introduction:

Prepare to go on a journey that combines old wisdom about financial prosperity with cutting- edge artificial intelligence (AI) capabilities. By combining ancient wisdom with cutting-edge technology, you'll discover a powerful method for improving your financial well-being. Follow these steps to navigate the intersection of traditional knowledge and artificial intelligence for a successful future.

1. **Accept Ancient Financial Principles:** Enter the realm of time-honored financial wisdom. Recognize the fundamental concepts of frugality, prudent investing, and resource management that guided our forefathers to prosperity.

2. **Understand AI's Analytical Capabilities:** Dive into the world of AI and learn about its ability to analyze massive volumes of data with unprecedented speed and precision. This technology can reveal patterns and trends that correspond to traditional financial principles.

3. **Incorporate Mindful Spending:** Bring the ancient practice of mindful spending into the digital era. Track your expenses, uncover possibilities for savings, and align your spending patterns with your financial goals with AI-powered budgeting tools.

4. **Predictive Financial Insights:** Use AI's predictive capabilities to anticipate prospective financial issues. AI can foresee market trends and guide strategic investment decisions in the same way that ancient societies did.

5. **Using AI to Automate Savings and Investments:** Use AI to automate your savings and investing strategies. Automate transfers to your savings account or utilize robo-advisors to make intelligent investing decisions that are in line with your objectives.

6. **Holistic Financial Well-being:** In ancient societies, well-being was thought to include all elements of life, including financial. Combine this perspective with AI-powered financial tools that provide detailed insights into your financial health.

7. **Navigating hazards with Insights:** Use AI to traverse financial hazards in the same way that ancient explorers did. AI can evaluate market data, assess risks, and provide ways for protecting your capital.

8. **Customized Financial Solutions:** Ancient wisdom was tailored to specific situations. Integrate artificial intelligence to receive personalized financial insights and solutions tailored to your specific goals, risk tolerance, and scenario.

9. **Ethical Considerations and AI:** As you embrace AI, keep ethical considerations and data privacy in mind. Ensure that AI applications correspond with your values and respect your privacy, much as ancient societies respected trust and integrity.

10. **Creating Your success Blueprint:** Combine old financial wisdom with AI-powered tools to create a financial success blueprint. Incorporate savings, spending, and investing ideas that resonate with both history and innovation.

Congratulations on successfully navigating the convergence of ancient financial wisdom and AI- powered tools. You are going on a transforming path toward financial wealth by following these instructions. Remember, you're constructing a tapestry that combines our forefathers' timeless ideas with the boundless possibilities of AI, creating a guide for navigating modern financial environments with wisdom and foresight.

Chapter16: Ancient Savings Practices and Modern Technology: A Unified Path to Financial Security

Prepare to discover the dynamic synergy between time-honored saving traditions and cutting- edge modern technologies. This chapter will lead you through the process of smoothly integrating old wisdom with the power of AI, paving the road for a secure financial future.

Follow these steps to discover a rich mine of savings tactics that span centuries, as well as how AI might improve these practices for a successful future.

1. **Embrace Ancient Wisdom:** Dive into the domain of time-tested savings strategies. Recognize the frugality, delayed pleasure, and disciplined spending habits that serve as the cornerstone of financial security.

2. **Understand the AI Advantage:** Immerse yourself in the field of artificial intelligence and its potential to alter the way you save. AI has the power to evaluate data, identify trends, and provide individualized insights that are in sync with ancient wisdom.

3. **Reviving Time-Honored Savings Methods:**Investigate the practices on which previous generations relied. These approaches, which range from saving aside a percentage of your salary to establishing a conscious approach to spending, provide the foundation of financial security.

4. **AI-Enhanced Savings Methods:** With AI-powered savings tactics, you can embrace the future. To maximize savings, use AI- powered tools to automate transfers to your savings account, evaluate spending

habits, and optimize your budget.

5. **Combining Tradition and Innovation:** For a thorough savings strategy, combine ancient concepts with modern instruments. Infuse artificial intelligence-driven insights into the time- honored practice of saving money, resulting in a harmonic blend of old and new.

6. **prediction Savings and Investing:** Transform the ancient art of foresight into AI-powered prediction capabilities. Use artificial intelligence to forecast expenses, forecast market trends, and inform investment decisions, assuring a solid financial future.

7. **Using AI for Smart Investments:** Leverage AI's analytical prowess to improve your investing decisions. AI can evaluate massive data sets, discover profitable opportunities, and make suggestions that are consistent with the principles of prudent wealth creation.

8. **Maintaining Discipline and Flexibility:** Practice saving discipline while enabling AI to fine- tune your approach. AI provides real-time insights into your financial health, ensuring that your savings strategies remain on track with your objectives.

9. **Ethical Considerations and Technology:** As you embrace AI, keep ethics in mind. Ensure that the AI technologies you use correspond with your beliefs and respect your privacy, just as ancient cultures did.

10. **Creating Your Financial stability Blueprint:** Combine old savings wisdom with AI-powered tools to create a financial stability blueprint. Incorporate conscious spending, disciplined saving, and data-driven decision-making concepts into your financial approach.

Conclusion: Congratulations on bridging the gap between time-tested savings strategies and AI innovation. By following these recommendations, you're setting a route for financial security that spans generations. Remember, as you weave old knowledge and modern technology together, you're building a tapestry that ensures your financial future while honoring the lessons of the past.

Chapter17: Legacy and Estate Planning:

Bridging Ancient Traditions and Artificial Intelligence Tools for Generational Wealth

Introduction:

Prepare to go on a journey that combines the timeless art of legacy creation with the efficiency of modern artificial intelligence techniques. This chapter will guide you through the maze of legacy and estate planning, seamlessly blending ancient traditions with cutting-edge technologies. Follow these steps to access the wisdom of previous generations and leverage AI's potential for generational wealth creation and preservation.

1. **Accept the Wisdom of Legacy Creation:** Enter the world of ancient traditions that recognized the value of legacy. Recognize that leaving a legacy involves more than just handing down monetary money; it also entails passing down values, wisdom, and a sense of purpose.

2. **Uncover the Power of AI Tools:** Investigate AI and its disruptive potential in the domain of estate planning. The ability of AI to process massive amounts of data and analyze complex financial scenarios can help to speed up the process of leaving a lasting legacy.

3. **Discover Ancient Legacy Traditions:** Investigate the traditions of ancient cultures that ensured their legacies survived. From narrative to skill transmission, these traditions demonstrate the entire approach to creating a legacy that lasts generations.

4. **AI-Assisted Estate Planning:** Embrace the current era with AI-powered estate planning tools. These technologies can help to speed up legal processes, examine tax ramifications, and provide insights into asset distribution, all while adhering to legacy creation standards.

5. **Combining Ancient Wisdom and AI Efficiency:** Combine the wisdom of legacy creativity with the efficiency of AI-powered technologies. Use technology to establish wills, distribute assets, and even leave digital legacies, fusing tradition and innovation.

6. **Ensure Legacy Continuity:** Because of meticulous planning, ancient legacies have survived through generations. Use AI to build strong structures that safeguard your legacy, ensuring that your values and wealth endure.

7. **AI-Enhanced Financial Literacy:** Use AI-powered financial literacy tools to empower future generations. Educate them on money management, investing, and legacy preservation so that they can pass on your financial wisdom.

8. **Generational Wealth:** Adopt the habit of creating and keeping generational wealth. Use artificial intelligence to examine investment opportunities, manage assets, and change tactics, allowing your wealth to grow over time.

9. **Ethical Considerations and AI:** Keep ethical considerations in mind as you handle the junction of tradition and technology. Ensure that AI applications correspond with your ideals and honor your legacy, much as ancient cultures did.

10. **Creating Your heritage Blueprint:** Combine ancient heritage knowledge with AI-powered tools to create a blueprint for generational prosperity. Incorporate the essence of heritage, values, and innovative tactics into your legacy planning.

Congratulations for bridging the gap between ancient legacy practices and AI-powered efficiency. By following these steps, you will embark on a transformative journey toward leaving a lasting impression that will stand the test of time. Remember that while you leave a legacy through the tapestry of tradition and technology, you are honoring the knowledge of the past while embracing the prospects of the future.

125

Chapter18: Financial Education and Continuous Learning:

Combining Ancient Wisdom with Artificial Intelligence for Lifelong Financial Evolution

Introduction:

Prepare to go on a journey that combines old financial teaching techniques with the dynamic powers of current AI. This chapter will help you navigate the world of financial learning and continuous improvement as you smoothly integrate historical insights with cutting-edge instruments of today. Follow these steps to unlock the knowledge vault and leverage AI's promise for lifetime financial evolution.

1. **Embrace Ancient Financial Education methods:** Enter the world of ancient financial education methods steeped in knowledge. Recognize the importance of developing financial literacy, which includes anything from bartering techniques to money management practices passed down through generations.

2. **Examine AI's function in current Financial Learning:** Examine AI and its revolutionary function in current financial education. AI's data-driven insights, individualized learning pathways, and interactive tools can transform your financial knowledge journey.

3. **Investigate past Financial Education Systems:** Examine the educational methods of past cultures that valued sharing financial knowledge. These practices promoted a common grasp of financial principles, from mentorship connections to community conversations.

4. **Personalized Learning with AI:** Use AI to personalize your financial learning journey. AI- powered platforms analyze your learning style, interests, and knowledge gaps to create a customized curriculum that is relevant to you.

5. **Integrating Ancient Wisdom and AI Precision:** Combine the age-old wisdom of financial education with the precision of AI. Utilize technology to gain access to resources, participate in simulations, and receive real-time feedback, thereby fusing tradition and contemporary.

6. **Lifelong Learning for Financial Evolution:** Ancient cultures valued knowledge acquisition throughout one's life. Integrate AI-powered technologies that keep you up to date on changing financial environments and methods to embrace lifelong learning.

7. **Skill Development and Financial Mastery:** Accept skill development as a technique of achieving financial mastery. Use artificial intelligence to identify skill gaps and give you with learning options that will help you on your financial journey.

8. **Financial Decision-Making Empowerment:** Use AI's analytical powers to improve your financial decision-making abilities. Understanding market trends and data-driven insights will help you make smarter investing decisions.

9. **Ethical Considerations and AI:** As you embark on your learning path with AI, keep ethical concerns in mind. Ensure that the AI technologies you use correspond with your beliefs and respect your privacy, just as ancient cultures did.

10. **Creating a Learning Blueprint:** Combine old financial education ideas with AI-powered tools to create a learning blueprint for ongoing learning. Integrate legacy and innovation to create a blueprint for lifelong financial evolution.

Congratulations on bridging the gap between historical financial education systems and the possibilities of AI. You are going on a transforming path toward continuous financial evolution by following these steps. Remember that as you traverse the junction of history and technology, you are weaving a tapestry that honors the wisdom of the past while welcoming the limitless possibilities of the present and future.

Chapter 19: Integrating Ancient Teachings with Artificial Intelligence for Holistic Prosperity

Prepare to go on a journey that mixes ancient wisdom teachings with breakthrough discoveries from current AI. This chapter will lead you through the junction of riches and spiritual growth, where age-old lessons collide with cutting-edge technology. Follow these methods to create a state of equilibrium between financial wealth and spiritual advancement, paving the way for general prosperity.

1. **Recognize Ancient Wealth and Spiritual Teachings:** Enter the world of ancient teachings that understood the delicate balance between affluence and spiritual development. Recognize that true prosperity entails both material wealth and inner fulfillment.

2. **Explore AI's Insights into Conscious Wealth Management:** Learn about the world of AI and how it can help you better comprehend conscious wealth management. The ability of AI to analyze data and trends can yield insights that correlate to your spiritual goals.

3. **Examine Ancient Wisdom on Prosperity and Spirituality:** Examine ancient wisdom that emphasized the link between prosperity and spirituality. From charitable giving to living in harmony with nature, these teachings highlight the harmony of material and metaphysical aspects of existence.

4. **AI-Enhanced Financial Insights:** Use AI-powered financial insights that align with your spiritual goals. AI may evaluate your financial patterns, propose ethical investing possibilities, and assist

you in making financial decisions that are in line with your values.

5. **Combining Ancient Wisdom and AI Precision:** Combine ancient wealth and spirituality teachings with AI precision. Use technology to assess your financial decisions, investments, and charitable efforts to ensure they are in harmony with your spiritual journey.

6. holistic well- being cannot be overstated. Use artificial intelligence to manage your finances in ways that prioritize spiritual and emotional development as well as financial achievement.

7. **AI-Powered Impactful Giving:** Make a major difference through philanthropic giving by leveraging AI's analytical capabilities. AI can identify causes that align with your values and provide data-driven insights to ensure that your efforts are meaningful.

8. **Mindful Financial Decisions:** Use AI to make conscious financial decisions that align with your spiritual path. Recognizing the ethical implications of your assets and spending can help you advance spiritually.

9. **Ethical Considerations and Artificial Intelligence:** When integrating technology with spirituality, keep ethics in mind. As ancient societies valued integrity, ensure that the AI tools you use align with your beliefs and respect your spiritual journey.

10. **Creating Your Holistic Wealth Blueprint:** Combine ancient financial and spiritual teachings with AI-powered tools to develop a holistic wealth blueprint. In order to establish a path that honors both sides of your existence, infuse intention into the material and spiritual spheres.

Finally, congratulations on successfully bridging the gap between traditional wealth teachings and new AI insights. By following these directions, you are embarking on a transformative journey toward holistic achievement. Remember that while you deal with the clash of tradition and technology, you're weaving a tapestry that balances material plenty with spiritual advancement, fostering a life that thrives in both dimensions.

Planning for retirement has changed over the years, mixing old ideas with new ones to help people get ready for life after work. Let's look at how all these parts fit together:

Principles from the Past:

Savings and Self-Sufficiency: Putting money aside for the future is an old idea. Throughout history, people from many different countries have stressed how important it is to save money for old age. In societies that were based on farming, people kept extra crops and things for times when they couldn't work as well or at all.

Intergenerational Support: In the past, when people retired, they often depended on strong family and community networks to help them out. Elders would be taken care of by their children or other family members, which would build a sense of duty between generations.

Saving money and Simplicity: In the past, many countries were frugal and made do with what they had. People often got used to living on less this way, which could make it easier for them to switch to a set income when they retire.

Techniques of today:

Financial Planning: Comprehensive financial methods are used in modern retirement planning. People work with financial advisers to figure out how much money they will need in retirement, set savings goals, and create investment portfolios that will bring in money during retirement.

Employer-Sponsored Retirement Plans: 401(k)s and pension plans, which are offered by companies, are common in modern countries. With these plans, employees can put away a portion of their pay, which is often matched by their company, to save money over the course of their careers.

Social Security and Government Programs: Social security and pension programs are a safety net for retirees in a lot of countries. These programs are meant to help people save more money and make sure they have a base standard of living.

Diversified investments: Modern retirement planning focuses on having diversified investment portfolios, which lower risk by spreading investments across different asset types like stocks, bonds, real estate, and more.

Longevity planning: Because of improvements in health care and longer life expectancies, people today have to plan for a longer time in retirement. This means that they need to carefully plan their finances to make sure that their savings will last through their retired years.

Healthcare Planning: The cost of health care can have a big effect on your finances in retirement. Modern planning for retirement takes into account the costs of medical care and may include things like health savings accounts (HSAs) and long-term care insurance.

Estate Planning: It's important to plan your estate so that your assets are given out according to your wishes after you die. Wills, trusts, and other legal tools are used in modern ways to handle your estate efficiently.

Bringing together ancient ideas and modern methods:

Planning for retirement today uses both old ideas and new ways of doing things. We still need to save money, be self-reliant, and help each other, but current tools and strategies make it easier to plan for a comfortable retirement. By putting these things together, people can make a retirement plan that takes into account their finances, their families, and their own needs.

Module 4:
The Journey to Wealth Creation

Chapter 20: Ancient Financial Milestones from the Past

Introduction: Join us on a fascinating journey through history as we investigate the financial milestones of ancient civilizations. This chapter acts as a time machine, transporting you to periods when economic foundations were laid and financial habits were established. Follow these steps to travel back in time and uncover the building pieces that built our present economic landscape.

1. **Barter Systems and Trade:** Travel back in time to when barter systems ruled human civilization. Discover how groups traded commodities and services based on mutual needs, laying the groundwork for economic engagement.

2. **Currency Evolution:** Observe the evolution of currency from shells and commodities to standardized forms such as coins and paper money. Discover how this breakthrough facilitated trade and laid the groundwork for current monetary systems.

3. **Agriculture and Surplus:** Investigate the role of agriculture in shaping economic systems. Learn how surplus food production facilitated specialization, commerce expansion, and the formation of societal hierarchies.

4. **Ancient Markets & Commerce:** Explore ancient civilizations' bustling marketplaces. Witness the meeting of merchants, artisans, and buyers, which promotes economic progress and cultural exchange.

5. **Banking Foundations:** Investigate the roots of banking in temples and royal treasuries. Discover how these organizations made loans, encouraged commerce, and even issued early kinds of currency.

6. **Trade Route Innovations:** Investigate the influence of ancient trade routes such as the Silk Road and Trans-Saharan trade. Consider how these routes linked cultures and allowed for the flow of products, ideas, and technologies.

7. **Ancient Empires' Monetary Policies:** Investigate the monetary policies of ancient empires such as Rome and China. Investigate how countries issued coinage, managed inflation, and developed fiscal restrictions.

8. **Landownership and Wealth:** Recognize the significance of land ownership in ancient societies. Consider how access to land and agriculture influenced social standing and wealth accumulation.

9. **The Origins of Credit:** Investigate the origins of credit systems in ancient cultures. Learn how merchants and dealers provided credit to facilitate transactions that required more than just cash.

10. **Legal and Financial Codifications:** See how ancient civilizations developed legal and financial rules. Learn how Hammurabi's Code and other legal systems laid the groundwork for commerce, contracts, and property rights.

11. **Early Financial Wisdom Lessons:** Consider the eternal financial lessons that ancient civilizations may impart to us. Discover how saving, risk management, and community support principles transcend ages.

12. **Present Parallels and Reflections:** Make comparisons between historical financial milestones and present economic systems. Consider how these historical lessons influence our financial practices now.

Conclusion: You have traveled through the early days of finance, witnessing the milestones that laid the road for our modern economic world. You've uncovered the roots of our financial systems by following these steps, acquiring insights that connect the past to the present.

Remember that by following in the footsteps of previous civilizations, you will obtain a better knowledge of the economic threads that connect our global society.

Mapping the Wealth Journey from the Beginning

Introduction:

Prepare to embark on a guided investigation of your wealth journey right from the start. This chapter will guide you through the essential stages of wealth acquisition and growth. Follow these steps to explore the map of your financial path, allowing you to make educated decisions and achieve your objectives.

1. **Basis and Mindset:** Begin your riches quest by creating a firm foundation. Develop a growth-oriented and positive mindset. Accept the idea that wealth is more than simply money and involves your thinking, habits, and values.

2. **Determining Financial Objectives:** Determine specific and attainable financial objectives. Your goals will be your guiding stars as you navigate the wealth journey, whether it's buying a home, starting a business, or achieving retirement security.

3. **Budgeting and Saving:** Learn how to budget and save money. Create a reasonable budget that allows you to allocate funds toward your goals while still saving for an emergency and investing.

4. **Debt Management:** Recognize the significance of debt management. Prioritize repayment of high-interest loans while being savvy about leveraging low-interest debts for investments.

5. **Investment Education:** Learn about the various investment opportunities available to you. Investigate stocks, bonds, real estate, and other investment options to make informed decisions that are consistent with your risk tolerance and financial objectives.

6. **Diversification:** Understand the investing diversification principle. To reduce risk and maximize profits, diversify your assets across industries and asset types.

7. **Retirement Planning**: Begin planning for your retirement as soon as possible. Investigate retirement account options and contribute consistently to ensure a solid financial future.

8. **Risk Assessment and Insurance:** Understand the function of insurance in protecting your assets. Investigate health, life, and property insurance to safeguard your possessions and loved ones.

9. **Tax Planning:** Learn about tax methods to improve your financial prospects. Learn ways to reduce your income, investments, and estate taxes.

10. **10, Ongoing Learning:** Commit to lifelong personal finance education. Maintain current knowledge of economic developments, investment opportunities, and financial best practices.

11. **Adjustment and Adaptation:** Recognize that the wealth journey is a living thing. Be ready to change your strategies when your circumstances change, and embrace flexibility and adaptation.

12. **Giving Back and Estate Planning:** Consider your impact on the community and future generations as you amass riches. Investigate charitable giving and legacy planning to leave a lasting legacy.

Conclusion:

Congratulations on mapping your wealth path from the beginning to an empowered future. By following these steps, you will be able to navigate each stage with confidence and clarity.

Remember that this is your journey; embrace it with an open mind, a willingness to learn, and the determination to reach your financial goals.

Chapter 21: Midlife Financial Strategies

Midlife involves serious financial preparation because it frequently marks peak earning years and a move toward thinking about retirement. Consider the following strategies:

Reevaluate Your Financial Goals: Examine your financial goals to see if they are in line with your current lifestyle and future ambitions. Maybe your priorities have altered since you last set those goals, and they need to be updated.

Increase Your Retirement Contributions: If you haven't been increasing your retirement contributions, now is the time. Employer matching, catch-up contributions (if you're over 50), and diversifying your retirement assets based on your risk tolerance are all options

Review Your Investment Portfolio: It's time to go over your portfolio and rebalance it. Make sure it corresponds to your risk tolerance, especially as you near retirement. Make sure your asset mix is diverse.

Pay Down Debt: Pay down high-interest debt first, especially credit card debt. If interest rates have fallen, look into refinancing alternatives for homes or student loans.

Create an Emergency Fund: If you haven't already, strive to have 6-12 months of living expenses set up for emergencies. This might provide you with piece of mind if unforeseen costs emerge.

Consider Long-Term Care Insurance: As you become older, the likelihood of needing healthcare increases. Long-term care insurance, which can cover expenditures that traditional health insurance or Medicare do not, may be a sensible investment right now.

Revise Your Estate Plan: If you haven't already, now is a great time to draft or revise your will, establish trusts, establish power of attorney, and create healthcare directives.

Plan for Your Children: This could entail saving for college, assisting them in their early professions, or contributing to the down payment on their first home. It's also a wonderful opportunity to teach kids about personal finance.

Plan for Aging Parents: As your parents get older, they may require financial or caregiving assistance. Talking openly with them about their financial situation and plans will help you prepare.

Rethink Your Housing Situation: Do you require a larger home, or is it time to downsize? Examine your existing and prospective housing requirements. If your children are leaving, you may discover that a smaller, more manageable room fits your lifestyle better.

Pursue Career Growth or move: Midlife might be a good time to look for promotions, raises, or even a career move. If you're feeling stuck, consider furthering your degree to increase your income potential.

Diversify Income Streams: Think about creating passive income streams. This could include purchasing real estate, launching a side business, or purchasing dividend-paying stocks.

Keep up to date: The financial landscape, tax rules, and investment opportunities all change over time. Read, attend classes, or talk with a financial counselor to stay informed.

Seek Professional Advice: If you haven't already done so, think about hiring a financial advisor. They can offer advice targeted to your unique circumstances and assist you in navigating the intricacies of midlife financial planning.

Remember that midlife is a period for introspection and action. Realigning your financial plans now can lay the groundwork for a more pleasant future, allowing you to enjoy the fruits of your labor in your retirement years.

Chapter 22: Retirement: Ancient Principles and Modern Techniques

Planning for retirement has changed over the years, mixing old ideas with new ones to help people get ready for life after work. Let's look at how all these parts fit together:

Principles from the Past:

Savings and Self-Sufficiency: Putting money aside for the future is an old idea. Throughout history, people from many different countries have stressed how important it is to save money for old age. In societies that were based on farming, people kept extra crops and things for times when they couldn't work as well or at all.

Intergenerational Support: In the past, when people retired, they often depended on strong family and community networks to help them out. Elders would be taken care of by their children or other family members, which would build a sense of duty between generations.

Saving money and Simplicity: In the past, many countries were frugal and made do with what they had. People often got used to living on less this way, which could make it easier for them to switch to a set income when they retire.

Techniques of today:

Financial Planning: Comprehensive financial methods are used in modern retirement planning. People work with financial advisers to figure out how much money they will need in retirement, set savings goals, and create investment portfolios that will bring in money during retirement.

Employer-Sponsored Retirement Plans: 401(k)s and pension plans, which are offered by companies, are common in modern countries. With these plans, employees can put away a portion of their pay, which is often matched by their company, to save money over the course of their careers.

Social Security and Government Programs: Social security and pension programs are a safety net for retirees in a lot of countries. These programs are meant to help people save more money and make sure they have a base standard of living.

Diversified investments: Modern retirement planning focuses on having diversified investment portfolios, which lower risk by spreading investments across different asset types like stocks, bonds, real estate, and more.

Longevity planning: Because of improvements in health care and longer life expectancies, people today have to plan for a longer time in retirement. This means that they need to carefully plan their finances to make sure that their savings will last through their retired years.

Healthcare Planning: The cost of health care can have a big effect on your finances in retirement. Modern planning for retirement considers the costs of medical care and may include things like health savings accounts (HSAs) and long-term care insurance.

Estate Planning: It's important to plan your estate so that your assets are given out according to your wishes after you die. Wills, trusts, and other legal tools are used in modern ways to handle your estate efficiently.

Bringing together ancient ideas and modern methods:

Planning for retirement today uses both old ideas and new ways of doing things. We still need to save money, be self-reliant, and help each other, but current tools and strategies make it easier to plan for a comfortable retirement. By putting these things together, people can make a retirement plan that considers their finances, their families, and their own needs.

Chapter23: Nurturing Prosperity and Harmony: Money's Role in Relationships

The interplay between money and relationships has always played an important role in the journey of human connection. Ancient teachings have provided insights into how money affect partnerships, and modern techniques such as artificial intelligence have enabled us to manage these dynamics more efficiently. This lecture investigates ancient wisdom and modern skills, offering advice on how to build money as a pair in harmony.

AI for Relationship Finance Management

In the financial sphere, the incorporation of AI has transformed how couples handle their money. Artificial intelligence-powered solutions may evaluate spending trends, generate budgets, and provide insights for improved financial decisions. This technology eliminates the need for human calculations as well as arguments caused by financial misconceptions. Couples can focus on strengthening their relationship while AI handles the difficulties of financial management.

A Harmonious Approach to Wealth Creation

Building and managing wealth as a partnership needs a fine balance of communication, trust, and mutual goals. Transparency and teamwork in financial matters are stressed in ancient teachings. Couples can lay the groundwork for their financial journey by harmonizing their ambitions and values. Setting mutual goals, such as homeownership, retirement plans, or travel ambitions, is part of the harmonic method.

Understanding individual money mindsets is also critical. According to ancient wisdom, various people have diverse attitudes regarding money, which are often molded by their upbringing and experiences. Couples can avoid possible disputes and build a shared financial goal by understanding their differences and working together to find common ground.

Financial harmony is built on effective communication. It is critical to have regular discussions regarding financial accomplishments, issues, and modifications. Open dialogues, according to ancient wisdom, develop understanding and prevent hatred from festering. When faced with financial failures or windfalls, dealing with them as a group deepens the bond.

Conclusion: the interplay between money and relationships is a timeless dance that evolves with the help of contemporary means. Couples can develop prosperity and harmony in their shared journey to building wealth by embracing AI for efficient financial management and weaving in ancient teachings on collaboration and understanding.

Chapter 24 The Symbiosis of Wealth and Ethics: Insights from the Past and AI

Ancient Ethical Wealth Norms

Civilizations throughout history have supported specific principles surrounding the ethical acquisition and utilization of riches. These norms are based on the belief that wealth, when acquired and handled wisely, may benefit society. Values such as charity, fairness, and the well- being of all are emphasized in ancient teachings. Exploring these principles lays the groundwork for understanding the complex link between money and ethics.

AI's View on Wealth and Ethics

The incorporation of AI into various parts of life in the modern period has extended to ethical questions surrounding wealth. AI algorithms can now evaluate investment opportunities, forecast market trends, and even advise on long-term financial decisions. This viewpoint illustrates the potential for AI to link wealth production with ethical ideals, proving that technology may be a valuable friend in navigating the complex environment of financial ethics.

Integrity and Wealth Creation

Integrity and wealth creation require a deliberate effort to sustain ethical beliefs while pursuing financial success. Individuals and businesses can establish strategies that prioritize long-term social well-being over short-term gains by drawing inspiration from ancient wisdom and leveraging AI discoveries. This integration demands adopting a responsible and empathic worldview, ensuring that wealth is earned and dispersed in ways that benefit both personal prosperity and the broader good.

This chapter explores how ethical considerations can be effortlessly integrated into wealth creation by merging the timeless wisdom of ethical wealth from the past with the novel insights afforded by AI. This comprehensive strategy benefits not just individuals and communities, but also lays the groundwork for a more ethical and sustainable future.

Chapter 25: Illuminating Asset Allocation: Combining Ancient Wisdom with Modern AI

The strategic deployment of assets acts as an indicator in the compelling journey towards wealth, drawing knowledge from the ages past and the intelligence of AI. In this chapter, we go on a revolutionary journey that combines ancient wisdom with cutting-edge technology to help you master the subtle art of asset allocation.

Asset Distribution Strategies for the Elderly

Follow in the footsteps of ancient civilizations that valued the balance and diversity of asset allocation. Consider their principles for allocating resources across domains, whether they are concrete assets like land or immaterial ones like knowledge. Consider how such insight can help to inform your own contemporary approach, building resilience and security.

Artificial Intelligence in Modern Asset Allocation

Consider the power that AI will have on your path. Consider algorithms that effortlessly navigate large oceans of data, revealing trends and giving improvement opportunities. Explore into AI's ability to transform your asset allocation journey, illuminating your route with smart decisions that could boost your returns and reduce risks.

Developing Asset Management Skills

Let us now engage on a revolutionary merger of the past and present in order to create a masterpiece of asset allocation. Begin by visualizing your goals, determining your risk tolerance, and aligning your investments with your values. Accept the rhythm of regular examination and modifications, as ancient cultures did while adapting to fluctuating tides.

To properly engage with the material and begin your enlightened road to prosperity, do the following:

Reflect: After each segment, pause to consider how ancient knowledge resonates with you and how AI might help you make better financial decisions.

Visualize: Close your eyes and imagine your financial goals becoming a reality, aided by a harmonic blend of time-tested concepts and cutting-edge innovation.

Plan: Create a personal asset allocation strategy that balances risk and return, pulling influence from both history and artificial intelligence.

Dialogue: Have talks with friends or mentors, discussing your thoughts from this chapter and learning from theirs.

Adapt: Both ancient societies and AI algorithms embrace the concept of flexibility. Maintain an open mind about fine-tuning your strategies as circumstances change.

In this chapter, "Illuminating Asset Allocation: Uniting Ancient Wisdom and Modern AI," you are at a historical and technological crossroads. When you study the material and put it into practice, you're not just learning about wealth building; you're experiencing a change that bridges the ages and puts you on a road of enlightened financial growth.

Chapter26: Creating Meaningful Legacies: Combining Timeless Wisdom with AI Guidance

The idea of leaving a meaningful legacy resonates across generations in the symphony of existence. This chapter takes you on a remarkable journey, merging the wisdom of ancient traditions with the potential of AI and helping you to create legacies that will last beyond your lifetime.

Ancient Legacy Preservation Traditions

Step into the shoes of our forefathers, who saw the fundamental importance of their acts resonating through time. Consider their rituals, myths, and cultural practices aimed at preserving their legacy. Consider how these traditions match with your own values and objectives, providing as timeless guidance to leave a lasting impression.

AI in Legacy Structure and Protection

Consider the possibilities as AI supports you in structuring and securing your legacy. Consider artificial intelligence's potential to organize massive amounts of data, produce interactive digital records, and even simulate discussions with future generations. Investigate AI's ability to transcend time, guaranteeing that your wisdom and goals endure and creating connections beyond ages.

Leaving a Long-Lasting Imprint

Combine old wisdom with modern innovation to create a legacy with depth and breadth. Begin by considering the meaning you want to communicate and matching your activities with your beliefs and objectives. Engage in open conversations with loved ones to better grasp their points of view and desires. Accept the essence of constant learning, reflecting both past and future wisdom.

To fully immerse yourself in the investigation of legacy creation:

Think: After each section, pause to reflect on the concept of legacy and its impact on your life and the lives of others you care about.

Journal: Write down your thoughts, dreams, and ideas regarding the legacy you want to leave behind, both as an individual and within your family or community.

Participate: Start talks with friends and family about legacy, pulling inspiration from their views and experiences.

Imagine: Imagine the long-term impact of your activities, inspired by the wisdom of ancient traditions and the promise of AI to carry your legacy on

Plan: Create a roadmap for your legacy that includes tangible activities and digital initiatives that combine prior wisdom and AI's capabilities.

In this chapter, "Crafting Legacies of Significance," you are encouraged to travel through time and explore the fascinating convergence of ancient wisdom and AI innovation. By working with this information, you will begin on a transforming journey of insight, action, and connection that will last centuries. Your legacy is more than simply a memory; it is a living witness to your ideals, formed by the interplay between tradition and technology.

Module 5:

Expanding Horizons: Global Perspectives on Wealth

Chapter 27: Global Wealth Navigating Through Time and Technology:

Lessons from Ancient Trade and AI

Explore the synergy between historic trade routes and cutting-edge AI capabilities as we go on a voyage that spans continents and epochs. In this chapter, you'll learn how historical trade paved the path for modern global prosperity and how artificial intelligence (AI) is continuing to transform the landscape of international trade and investment.

The Silk Road: An Ancient Global Trade Model

Set off on the Silk Road's route, a testament to humanity's innate thirst for connection and prosperity. Consider the long-distance flow of goods, ideas, and civilizations that laid the groundwork for globalization. Consider how these ancient trading routes provide lessons into bridging borders and cultures, encouraging shared wealth and understanding.

Artificial Intelligence in Modern Global Trade and Investment

Consider a scenario in which AI algorithms evaluate large amounts of data, forecast market trends, and optimize international trade and investment strategies. Dive into the world of AI- powered supply chain management, risk assessment, and real-time decision-making to realize the enormous potential for streamlining and improving the global economic environment.

Using Global Perspectives to Increase Local Wealth

Now, combine the wisdom of old trade with the accuracy of artificial intelligence to create a plan for local wealth in a global setting. Begin with comprehending how cultures, economies, and technologies interact in today's interconnected world. Participate in cross-cultural discourse and collaboration, inspired by the spirit of ancient traders who linked many civilizations.

To fully immerse oneself in this investigation of global wealth:

Explore: Learn about ancient trade routes other than the Silk Road to have a better grasp of how global trade has shaped civilizations.

Analyze: After each segment, consider how old trade lessons and AI advancements may be applied to your personal financial strategy.

Connect with: Participate in online forums or networking events centered on international commerce and investment, where you may share views and learn from global viewpoints.

Strategize: Integrate artificial intelligence (AI) tools into your financial decision-making process, employing their analytical skills to improve global investment plans.

Imagine: Consider a world in which you participate to cross-border collaboration and economic growth, fueled by the old spirit of traders and aided by artificial intelligence.

As you read "Navigating Global Wealth Through Time and Technology," you'll be invited to bridge the past and present, cultivating a mindset that welcomes global interconnection while maximizing AI's possibilities. Your participation in this material equips you to manage the intricacies of today's global economy, paving your own route to wealth and connection in an ever-changing world.

Chapter 28: Unveiling Cultural Dimensions of Wealth:

A Meeting of Ancient Wisdom and AI

Begin a captivating journey that crosses countries and periods, diving into the rich tapestry of different viewpoints on wealth. This chapter will guide you through the intricate threads weaved by ancient civilizations and highlighted by artificial intelligence, providing fascinating insights into global financial principles and practices.

Ancient Wealth Perspectives from Different Cultures

Explore the varied landscapes of human civilizations, where different cultures have bestowed their own views on wealth. Consider the teachings of several historic societies, from Eastern philosophies' notions of sufficiency and harmony to Western ideologies' quest of prosperity and honor. Consider how these cultural perspectives continue to influence our concept of wealth today.

Artificial Intelligence Insights into Modern Cultural Economic Models

Consider AI to be a cultural bridge, crossing borders and understanding the economic complexities of other nations. Learn how artificial intelligence-driven data analysis reveals cultural variations in spending habits, investing choices, and financial behaviors. Investigate AI's ability to detect patterns that illustrate how cultural values influence modern economic decisions.

Global Financial Values and Practices

Now, combine the knowledge of many cultures with AI's analytical prowess to chart a course that honors tradition while embracing innovation. Begin by building cultural curiosity by immersing yourself in stories and activities from around the world. Investigate how artificial intelligence (AI) can be used to bridge the gap between global values and localized financial strategies, promoting mutual understanding and shared success.

To fully connect with the content and embark on a profound cultural trip, follow these steps:

Immerse: After each segment, take a moment to analyze how the cultural viewpoints discussed resonate with your own financial principles.

Research: Read books, watch films, and read articles about different cultures' financial habits to extend your awareness of wealth's various meanings.

Dialogue: Discuss financial ideas and practices with friends or colleagues from other cultural backgrounds, sharing insights and learning about their financial views and practices.

Adopt: Modify your financial strategy to include elements from different cultures that speak to you, guided by the wisdom of both ancient teachings and modern AI insights.

Empathize: Imagine yourself in the shoes of people from other cultures, seeing their financial journeys and comprehending the impact that cultural values play in molding their financial decisions.

As you read "Unveiling Cultural Dimensions of Wealth," you will go on a transformative journey that embraces variety while embracing unity. Your interaction with this content promotes a greater awareness for the intricate tapestry of global financial viewpoints, providing you with a rich canvas on which to paint your own financial path.

Chapter 29: Currency Evolution: From Barter to Blockchain

Set out on a thrilling millennia-long journey that traces the evolution of currency from barter systems to the digital age of blockchain. This chapter untangles the historical strands and AI- powered insights that weave the complicated tapestry of currency, providing a glimpse into the future where history and technology meet.

Currency and Trade System History

Back in time, barter systems encouraged trading in ancient marketplaces. Consider the inventive origins of commodity money and early forms of currency such as cowrie shells and metal coins. Investigate how these structures facilitated commerce and collaboration, laying the groundwork for modern economies.

Artificial Intelligence in Modern Cryptocurrencies and Blockchain

Fast forward to the digital era, where artificial intelligence advancements are reinventing cash via cryptocurrencies and blockchain. Investigate the transformational power of blockchain's decentralized ledger and the complex mathematics that govern cryptocurrencies. Discover AI's role in forecasting cryptocurrency trends and allowing secure transactions, adding a contemporary spin to the monetary tale.

The Future of Currency: A Convergence of History and Technology

Imagine a future in which cash crosses physical and digital barriers, drawing on historical knowledge and propelled by AI. Consider the possibilities of a uniform global currency that reflects the collaborative spirit of barter systems while embracing blockchain technology's efficiency. Consider how artificial intelligence (AI) could transform economic landscapes, promoting prosperity and innovation.

To fully participate in this illuminating trip through the evolution of currency:

Picture: After each section, picture the evolution of cash from barter to blockchain and **how it**

Relates to your understanding of financial systems.

Remain Informed: Explore further into the world of cryptocurrencies and blockchain technology, staying up to date on the newest trends, breakthroughs, and controversies.

Experiment: If you are comfortable, try owning and trading in cryptocurrencies, gaining direct experience with the convergence of old concepts and modern technology.

Connect: Participate in communities, online forums, or local gatherings to explore the future of cash, exchange ideas, and widen your horizons.

Reflect: Take a minute to consider how currency evolution connects with your personal financial journey and ideals, incorporating insights from both the past and technology.

You travel through time as you read the chapter "Currency's evolution" seeing the evolution of currency from its humble beginnings to the frontiers of technology. Your interaction with this material leads you to a better knowledge of the complicated web that ties currency, history, and innovation, empowering you to navigate the future with a distinct blend of ancient wisdom and technical prowess.

Chapter 30: Investing Across Borders:

Combining Ancient Wisdom with AI Insights

Set out on a sublime journey that spans continents and epochs, revealing the synergy between age-old investment tactics and AI's technological power. This chapter walks you through the complex fabric of global investments, demonstrating how history and innovation intersect to build modern cross-border portfolios.

Cross-Border Investing: Ancient Global Investment Strategies

Follow in the footsteps of history's adventurous investors as they traveled unexplored waters in search of returns across distant regions. Consider the trade routes that shaped fortunes, where risk and reward interacted on a global scale. Explore the value of diversification as civilizations balanced their portfolios with a mix of rare products and economic concepts from other lands.

AI and Cross-Border Investments: Beyond Borders Insights

Advance into the age of artificial intelligence, when algorithms analyze massive datasets, find hidden patterns, and provide real-time insights for global investments. Discover how artificial intelligence may be used to assess cross-border markets, forecast currency swings, and prevent risks.

Investigate how artificial intelligence (AI) crosses geographical divides by transforming data into usable recommendations for people navigating today's interconnected financial landscape.

Bridging the Gap Between Traditional and Modern for a Global Portfolio

Now, combine traditional investment concepts with artificial intelligence's analytical precision to create a global investment portfolio that transcends boundaries and epochs. Begin by immersing yourself in the histories of other economies, becoming acquainted with their rhythms and potential. Participate in discussions with experts and peers, exchanging views that combine legacy with cutting-edge technology.

To interact with the content and begin your worldwide investment trip, follow these steps:

Reflect: Consider how ancient investment ideas resonate with AI-driven cross-border insights and how they may be implemented into your own portfolio after each section.

Educate: Learn about diverse locations' and cultures' investment history, improving your awareness of global markets and economic trends.

Network: Meet with professionals in the global finance industry to exchange ideas about cross-border investments and learn from their experiences.

Experiment: If suitable, consider incorporating overseas assets into your portfolio, drawing on both old wisdom and artificial intelligence's data-driven counsel.

Plan: Create a worldwide investing strategy that aligns with your financial goals and considers historical viewpoints and AI-generated insights.

As you read through the chapter "Investing Across Borders," you learned transformative adventure that crosses borders and time periods. By engaging with this content, you develop a global perspective, allowing ancient wisdom and AI-driven insights to affect your investment decisions and charting a course toward a cross-border portfolio that is founded in tradition and propelled by innovation.

Chapter 31: Philanthropy Unveiled: Weaving Timeless Compassion and AI-Powered Impact

As we explore the core of global philanthropy, we will travel across continents and cultures. This chapter explores the rich tapestry of giving practices throughout history, as well as the revolutionary possibilities of artificial intelligence in modern humanitarian activities. We will investigate how the convergence of traditional compassion and cutting-edge technology is transforming the landscape of global giving.

Global Giving Traditions in Philanthropy

Enter the historical record of human compassion, where giving has been a common language throughout history. Consider the various charitable practices, from ancient tribes' almsgiving to empires' endowments. Consider how these acts of compassion have endured through centuries and served as a foundation for modern charity activities.

Global Philanthropy History

Travel through time to see how societies embraced the spirit of giving to meet societal concerns. Learn how historical people and movements set the way for today's charity organizations. Look into the stories of individuals who made unforgettable contributions to the world via their selflessness.

Artificial Intelligence in Modern Charitable Ventures

To the present day, AI augments the influence of philanthropy in unprecedented ways. Discover how artificial intelligence-powered data analysis detects important societal concerns, optimizes resource allocation, and streamlines fundraising efforts. Investigate how technology has crossed borders, enabled worldwide collaboration and expanding the scope of charity endeavors.

To fully participate in this investigation of the evolution of philanthropy:

Reflect: Pause after each segment to contemplate how the stories of global giving inspire your own charitable journey.

Research: Explore deeper into the biographies of famous donors to learn about the motivations behind their philanthropy and the influence they had.

Connect: Participate in philanthropic online forums or local events, exchanging ideas and learning about others' experiences.

Act: Consider getting involved in philanthropic projects, employing AI tools to increase your impact, and contributing to causes that are important to you.

Imagine: Imagine a future in which AI and compassionate giving effortlessly integrate, revolutionizing the world of philanthropy and extending assistance to previously untapped areas of the globe.

As you read through the chapter "Philanthropy Unveiled," you become a part of the giving tapestry, weaving together the threads of ancient compassion and modern ingenuity. Your participation in this material enables you to embrace humanity's humanitarian history, motivated by both past acts of compassion and the revolutionary potential of AI.

Chapter 32: Financial Institutions Across Time and Technology:

A Fusion of Ancient and Modern

Set out on an enthralling journey that spans ages and digs into the formation of financial institutions. This chapter reveals the dynamic interplay between ancient roots and cutting-edge AI technology, demonstrating how banking and investment organizations have evolved over time.

Contextual Evolution of Ancient and Modern Financial Institutions

Enter the historical corridors where the seeds of financial institutions were sown. Consider the roots of lending, banking, and investment activities in different civilizations. Consider how these early systems created the framework for the sophisticated institutions that underpin the global economy today.

The Evolution of Financial Institutions: A Progress Tapestry

Travel through time, following the evolution of financial institutions from their humble beginnings to the sophisticated architecture of today. Witness the establishment of stock exchanges, the growth of central banks, and the introduction of contemporary banking methods. Investigate the resilience, ingenuity, and adaptation stories that have formed the financial world.

Artificial Intelligence in Modern Banking and Investment Firms: Redefining Possibilities

Transition to the current era, when artificial intelligence acts as a transformational beacon for financial institutions. Discover the power of AI-driven algorithms to improve risk assessment, improve customer experience, and transform investment strategies. Discover how technology has reshaped the landscape, hastening financial transactions and decision-making.

Financial Institutions' Future: A Harmonious Convergence

Consider a future in which the wisdom of ancient financial concepts meets AI-powered innovation. Consider the possibility of frictionless transactions, improved security, and personalized banking services. Consider how the marriage of old and new can reposition financial institutions as inclusive, efficient, and adaptive economic stability pillars.

To fully immerse oneself in this financial institution journey:

Reflect: After each session, pause to contemplate how financial institutions have evolved and how historical insights might impact your knowledge of modern finance.

Explore: Dive into the histories of well-known financial institutions to gain a better knowledge of their evolution and contributions to the financial world.

Participate: Take part in talks or events about the future of finance, sharing views and learning about the junction of tradition and technology.

Experiment: Embrace technology by using AI-powered financial services and witnessing the convergence of old and new in your financial transactions firsthand.

Plan: Create a financial strategy that aligns with your aims and ideals by incorporating both historical ideas and AI-driven breakthroughs.

As you progress through the chapter "Financial Institutions Through Time and Technology," you will encounter the shifting currents that have molded the financial world. Your participation in this material enables you to bridge the gap between the past and the present, respecting the foundations while embracing the chances that AI technology offers to improve the world of finance.

Module 6

Future of Finance and AI

Chapter 33: The AI Revolution in Finance:

Innovation and AI on the Rise

Step into the whirlwind of innovation where artificial intelligence (AI) is transforming banking through fintech. Consider how algorithms influence trade, lending, and consumer interactions. Consider the rapid evolution of AI-driven systems that provide streamlined financial services and personalized experiences, ushering in a new era of banking.

Uncharted Waters: Potential Threats and Ethical Concerns

Navigate the complexities of AI's rise, recognizing potential risks and ethical quandaries that arise. Look into debates concerning algorithmic bias, data privacy, and the displacement of established roles. Examine the delicate balance between automation and human control, as well as how social values can influence AI's path in banking.

Guiding the Revolution: Ensuring AI's Long-Term Role in Finance

Now, chart a course for a future in which AI's involvement in finance is not just innovative but also sustainable. Consider the importance of open algorithms, fair lending processes, and ethical decision-making. Investigate the possibility of regulatory systems that foster innovation while preventing unexpected consequences.

To fully immerse yourself in the investigation of the AI revolution in finance:

Educate: After reading each section, educate yourself on various fintech platforms, AI-powered financial services, and ethical debates around AI in finance.

Discuss: Engage in discussions with peers, mentors, or finance professionals, exchanging perspectives on AI's revolutionary impact and the ethical concerns it poses.

Evaluate: Examine your personal financial practices and interactions with AI-powered platforms, weighing the pros and hazards.

Advocate: Take part in conversations regarding artificial intelligence legislation and ethical principles, arguing for measures that promote responsible AI use in finance.

Plan: Develop a financial strategy that incorporates AI-driven tools while adhering to ethical principles, aligning with your beliefs, and contributing to a financially sustainable landscape.

As you progress through the chapter "Unleashing the AI Revolution in Finance," you will start on a journey of both discovery and responsibility. Your participation in this material enables you to embrace the positive features of AI while critically examining its possible problems, guiding you toward a future in which AI acts as a driver for financial success while respecting ethical issues and human values.

Chapter 34: Future Financial Products

The financial landscape is fast changing as we go deeper into the digital age. Let's peek at what future financial goods might look like:

1. Decentralized Finance (DeFi) Platforms *Yield Farming Platforms: * These will allow users to earn returns on their crypto assets by lending them.

Decentralized Exchanges (DEXs): These platforms enable peer-to-peer asset exchanges without the use of intermediaries.

2. Tokenized Assets *Real Estate Tokens:* On blockchain networks, properties can be tokenized, allowing individuals to hold portions of real estate assets.

Tokenized Art and Collectibles: Tokenized art and collectibles can be transferable on digital marketplaces.

3. Personalized Financial Robots: Using artificial intelligence, these robots will deliver personalized financial advice, investment plans, and tax planning based on an individual's personal and financial status.

4. Insurance and Smart Contracts Parametric Insurance: Using smart contracts on blockchain systems, this is a type of insurance that pays out when a specified condition or parameter is met.

5. AI-Enabled Predictive Investment Tools: These systems will evaluate massive volumes of data in order to forecast market moves and recommend investment strategies.

6. Digital Wallets Using Post-Quantum Cryptography: With the development of quantum computers, better cryptography approaches will be required to secure digital assets.

7. Holistic Financial Health Platforms: Platforms that mix traditional banking, investment, insurance, and even health and wellness counseling in one location, using data to deliver holistic financial and overall well-being guidance.

8. Platforms for Green and Sustainable Investment: Platforms dedicated to green bonds, sustainable projects, and ESG (Environmental, Social, and Governance) investments will grow as the emphasis on climate change and sustainability grows.

9. Universal Digital Identities: A single digital ID might be used for a variety of reasons, including banking authentication and access to public services.

10. Programmable Money: Central Bank Digital Currencies (CBDCs) and other types of digital money might be designed to only be spent for certain objectives, increasing the effectiveness of fiscal policies.

11. Retirement Options for the Gig Economy: With the advent of gig workers, new retirement and pension plans will emerge that are tailored to their specific financial circumstances.

12. Peer-to-Peer (P2P) Lending: The next generation of P2P lending will use AI and blockchain to provide more accurate risk assessment and globally connected lending networks.

Difficulties Ahead

While these technologies have the potential to transform the financial landscape, issues including regulatory barriers, privacy concerns, and the digital divide must be addressed. An inclusive approach that ensures everyone has access to the most up-to-date financial products, combined with global regulatory collaboration, will be critical in achieving the full potential of these technologies.

Chapter 35: Financial Education in the Age of Artificial Intelligence

Introduction

As financial systems get more complicated, so must the education that surrounds them. From ancient coinage and ledgers to today's algorithms and AI, how we teach and learn about finance has changed dramatically. This chapter will examine the evolution of financial education as well as the critical role AI is playing in developing a financially literate society.

Traditional Financial Education Methods

Financial education was founded on real-world experiences and traditional learning methods prior to the advent of digital simulations and e-learning modules.

Apprenticeships: Those interested in trade, banking, or commerce were traditionally trained as apprentices, learning the ins and outs of finance from seasoned experts.

Lessons on the Barter System: Individuals acquired the subjective value of items and the art of negotiation firsthand in early societies that relied on barter.

Storytelling:Ancient civilizations employed storytelling to transmit financial wisdom, such as the Greeks with their Midas stories or the Chinese with their money-related proverbs.

Artificial Intelligence's Role in Financial Literacy Programs

With the introduction of artificial intelligence, there is a revolution in how financial education is approached, making it more accessible, personalized, and dynamic.

Personalized Learning Pathways: AI algorithms assess a person's learning style and pace, then adapt financial courses to ensure optimal comprehension.

In the AI age, financial education is a synthesis of old wisdom and cutting-edge technology. A balanced and comprehensive financial education can be achieved by grounding teachings in historical context while providing learners with the tools to navigate an AI-driven financial landscape. Adaptability and lifelong learning will be the cornerstones of financial literacy as the barriers between technology and finance continue to blur.

Chapter 36: The Wealth and Happiness Relationship

Introduction

The eternal pursuit of happiness has frequently been connected with the goal of prosperity. From ancient philosophers debating the significance of material wealth in a happy existence to current artificial intelligence shedding light on the intricacies of wealth and well-being, the relationship between money and happiness has long been a source of debate.

Ancient Wealth and Contentment Philosophies

Historical wisdom provides a rich tapestry of viewpoints on the relationship of riches and happiness.

Stoicism (1.1): Stoics such as Seneca and Epictetus felt that while wealth is not intrinsically bad, it should not be a source of attachment. True contentment comes from knowing what we can control and accepting what we can't.

Buddhism: Material prosperity is viewed as a transient source of happiness rather than the ultimate source of happiness. According to Buddhist teachings, true happiness stems from inner calm, enlightenment, and the absence of wants.

Confucianism: Wealth is not frowned upon in Confucian ideology if earned ethically and used wisely. It highlights the rich's moral obligations to community peace and welfare.

Aristotelian Point of View: Wealth, according to Aristotle, was required but not sufficient for happiness. The ultimate ideal was 'eudaimonia,' or 'flourishing,' with riches being only one of its components.

Artificial Intelligence Insights on Modern Wealth and Well-Being.

The age of data and artificial intelligence provides new insights on the age-old subject of wealth's role to happiness.

Data Mining: According to studies based on large data sets, while a rise in money can contribute to an increase in happiness, it has decreasing returns. After a certain point, additional wealth has little effect on general well-being.

AI-Assisted Surveys: Artificial intelligence-powered platforms can now collect real-time data on people's emotional states, correlating financial decisions or milestones with immediate emotional responses.

Predictive Modeling:** AI algorithms may now forecast future well-being based on financial decisions, leading people to make decisions that will lead to their long-term satisfaction.

Creating a Meaningful Financial Journe

Individuals can design a financial journey that coincides with genuine contentment by using lessons from both old wisdom and modern technologies.

Materialism and Beyond: Recognizing that wealth is a means to an objective rather than an end. Wealth can bring comfort, stability, and opportunity, but wealth is not the only factor that determines pleasure.

Financial Awareness: Spending and investing can be aligned with personal values and long- term goals by being more attentive of financial actions and their effects.

Balance: . Finding a happy medium between living in the moment and planning for the future can lead to a rewarding financial journey. It entails comprehending the trade-offs between short-term joys and long-term fulfillment.

Giving and Community: Both ancient and modern ideologies emphasize the joy of giving. Contributing to the community, assisting others, and using riches for a greater good can all considerably improve well-being.

Conclusion

The connection between wealth and happiness is complex and deeply personal. While riches can offer means, true happiness is typically found in recognizing one's place in the larger scheme of things. Individuals find a compass to chart their routes to fulfillment in the intersection of historical ideologies and modern AI breakthroughs.

Module 7:

Financial Independence and Personal Growth

Chapter 37: Financial Independence Philosophy

Introduction

Financial independence, sometimes known as FI, has become a modern concept for those seeking freedom from the cyclical cycle of earning and spending. Financial independence is, at its root, the expression of freedom, choice, and personal fulfillment. This chapter digs into the meaning of FI, its historical roots, and its tremendous psychological effects.

An Overview of Financial Ind ependence (FI)

Definition and Summary:

Financial independence is reached when a person has amassed enough cash to cover living expenses without actively working or relying on a regular income. For many, the ultimate goal is "retiring early," sometimes known as the FIRE (Financial Independence, Retire Early) movement.

The FI Spectrum:

Financial security is not a one-size-fits-all idea. It occurs on a scale, ranging from basic financial stability, in which fundamental necessities are covered, to total financial wealth, in which one can live a luxurious lifestyle without working.

FI's Historical Context

Ancient Ideas:

The concept of amassing enough resources to be free of everyday toil was not foreign to ancient civilizations ranging from Greece to China. Philosophers such as Epicurus advocated in ancient Greece about living a simple life free of needless cravings and pursuing natural and necessary prosperity.

The Renaissance and the Age of Enlightenment:

The rise of new wealth, typically distinct from royalty or land, sparked debates over the right use of wealth and the concept of leisure during these periods. The concept of accumulating wealth while focusing on personal hobbies became more popular.

Modern Trends:

The 20-21 centuries saw the emergence of literature as well as movements centered on early retirement and inexpensive living.

The Psychological Importance of FI

Autonomy and Freedom:

At its core, FI provides a psychological break from society norms of working into old age. It allows people to follow their passions, hobbies, or even different occupations without the weight of financial obligations.

Less Financial Stress:

Several research have found a correlation between financial difficulties and psychological suffering. Achieving FI entails removing a large source of anxiety, which leads to greater mental health.

Control and Empowerment:

Financial freedom gives people a sense of control over their lives. It enables decisions to be driven by real curiosity and passion rather than financial need.

Personal Development:

Many people discover possibilities for personal growth with the newfound time and freedom that FI provides, whether it's acquiring new skills, traveling, or delving deeply into personal passions.

Conclusion

Financial freedom, while frequently depicted in monetary terms, transcends statistics. It reflects a life philosophy oriented on autonomy, personal progress, and freedom from financial commitments. As society advances and the FI movement grows, it begs the question, "What does true wealth and a fulfilled life mean to each of us?"

Chapter 38: The Blueprint for Financial Independence

Introduction

The journey to financial independence (FI) necessitates more than simply aspiration; it requires a sound roadmap. This chapter equips readers with the tools and knowledge they need to move from financial desire to realization by providing actionable insights into the essential building elements of FI.

The FI Foundations: Budgeting, Saving, and Investing

Budgeting:

Practical Example: Begin by keeping note of every penny you spend for a month. To organize and see your costs, use budgeting programs such as Mint or YNAB (You Need A Budget). After you've determined where your money is going, create a budget that prioritizes savings and necessary expenses.

Practical Example: Use the "pay yourself first" strategy. Before paying any bills, put a specific part of your salary (20% is a decent beginning point) into a separate savings account. Aim to increase this percentage over time.

Savings:

Practical Example: Begin with employer-sponsored retirement plans, maximizing any matching contributions. Consider index funds or ETFs to diversify your portfolio. If you're new to the stock market, automated advisors like Betterment or Wealth Front can help you automate investments based on your risk tolerance.

The Value of an Emergency Fund

Definition: An emergency fund is a collection of funds set aside to handle unexpected expenses such as medical problems or job loss.

Practical Example: Saving three to six months' worth of expenses in a liquid account, such as a high-yield savings account, is a good goal. Begin with a small target, such as $1,000, then work your way up. Set up automatic contributions to this fund every month until you attain your goal.

Passive Income Streams: The Golden Ticket to Financial Independence

Investing in Real Estate:

Practical Application: Think about investing in rental homes. Platforms such as Fundraise, and REITs (Real Estate Investment Trusts) can also provide exposure to real estate markets without requiring actual property ownership.

Dividend Stocks:

Practical Example: Invest in stocks that provide dividends. Dividends should be reinvested to maximize compound growth. Apps such as Robinhood or M1 Finance can be a fantastic place to start for beginning investors.

Develop Digital Products

Practical Example: Consider generating online courses, eBooks, or downloadable software if you have experience in a specific area. Platforms such as Udemy, Gumroad, and Teachable can help with this.

Conclusion

Financial independence is not reserved for a select few but is attainable by everyone with the necessary knowledge and dedication. By understanding the fundamental principles of budgeting, saving, and investing, as well as generating strong emergency funds and leveraging the power of passive income, the FI dream becomes progressively attainable. The first step, as with any journey, is sometimes the most difficult, but with this plan in hand, the route to financial independence becomes clearer and more feasible.

Chapter 39: Personal Development Through Financial Education

Introduction

Financial education is a critical pillar in the vast road of human development. It not only provides individuals with the knowledge to manage their resources, but it also provides a broader perspective of the world. This chapter explores the transforming aspect of financial literacy, its empowering impacts on decision-making, and inspirational stories from those who have succeeded as a result of financial education.

The Evolution of Financial Literacy

Financial literacy does not remain static; rather, it evolves in parallel with global economic upheavals, technological advancements, and societal requirements. The extent of financial knowledge has expanded enormously, from the primitive barter system to intricate stock market techniques.

The need of remaining up to date has never been more obvious in recent times, with the emergence of digital currencies, peer-to-peer lending platforms, and online financial tools. The dynamic character of financial literacy emphasizes the importance of ongoing learning and adaptation.

How Financial Education Facilitates Individual Decision-Making

Understanding money is only one aspect of a solid understanding of financial fundamentals. It shapes a person's mindset.

Financial education develops critical thinking skills. Individuals learn to evaluate chances not only in terms of immediate enjoyment, but also in terms of long-term rewards. They learn to distinguish between needs and wants and make decisions that are in line with their long-term goals.

Furthermore, those with financial understanding can decode the often-intimidating jargon of the finance sector, allowing them to engage in informed talks with professionals and ensuring they are not easily deceived.

Empowerment via financial education reveals itself in risk management as well. Individuals may measure the possible risks and rewards of financial enterprises with a foundational understanding, resulting in balanced and educated judgments.

Case Studies: Financial Education Success Stories

Jane's Path from Debt to Prosperity:

Jane was trapped and scared when she was buried behind a pile of credit card debt. But her life changed when she resolved to financially educate herself. Her education, which ranged from understanding interest rates to embracing frugal living, led her not only to pay off her debts but also to launch a thriving internet business.

Alex and the Stock Market:

Alex, a college student, happened to come across a book about stock market investing. This initial spark sparked his interest in financial books. He had a diverse portfolio by the time he graduated, creating a passive income stream and insuring his financial stability right out of college.

Lisa's Non-Profit Project:

Lisa wanted to start a non-profit organization because she was passionate about community involvement. She recognized, however, that passion alone would not enough. She mastered grant writing, budget management, and fundraising methods via focused financial study, transforming her non-profit idea into a community-changing reality.

Conclusion

Personal development and financial education are inextricably interwoven. Individuals who engage on a search for knowledge not only open doors to financial success, but also to a greater grasp of life's complexities. Thus, financial education is a transforming journey that enhances life in a variety of ways.

Chapter 40: Investment as a Financial Growth Tool

Introduction

Investment stands out as a significant driver for wealth multiplication in the large ecosystem of financial instruments. Investing, as opposed to simply saving, puts your money to work for you by using the power of compound interest and market dynamics. This chapter aims to illuminate the fundamental concepts of investment, the art of risk management, and a glance into the attractive investment paths of the future.

Investment Fundamentals: From Stocks to Real Estate

The allocation of resources, typically money, with the goal of earning an income or profit is known as investment. In this section, we'll look at two major areas: equities and real estate.

Stocks: Represent a portion of a company's ownership. When you acquire stock in a corporation, you are purchasing a portion of that company. Stocks are divided into three types: shares, bonds, and mutual funds. The stock market has enormous growth potential, particularly when assets are kept for a longer period of time.

Real estate is one of the oldest investment types. It entails purchasing physical property, such as land or buildings, with the idea that the value will increase or that the property will create rental income. While it often necessitates a greater initial investment, real estate can provide consistent profits and tax benefits.

Risk management is the process of balancing potential gains with security.

Every investment has some level of risk. Understanding and managing these risks, on the other hand, can make the difference between potential losses and strong financial growth.

Diversification is the practice of spreading investments over several types of assets, lessening the impact of a poor-performing investment on the total portfolio. It is also referred to as "not putting all your eggs in one basket."

Education and research: Keeping up with market trends, understanding business financials for stock investments, and researching localities for real estate purchases can all help to reduce risks.

Financial Advisors: For individuals who are unfamiliar with the subtleties of investing, financial advisors can provide specialized counsel, ensuring that your investment choices correspond with your risk tolerance and financial goals.

Investment Trends and Opportunities in the Future

The investing landscape is continually changing as a result of technological advances, societal shifts, and global events.

Cryptocurrencies: Digital currencies such as Bitcoin and Ethereum have exploded in popularity. While volatile, they offer a new financial frontier enabled by blockchain technology.

Sustainable Investing: With a global emphasis on sustainability, there is increased interest in investments in eco-friendly technologies, renewable energy, and sustainable agriculture.

Emerging Markets: Countries such as India, Brazil, and parts of Africa are experiencing significant economic growth, providing fertile ground for infrastructure, technology, and consumer goods investment.

Tech Innovations: Exciting investment prospects abound in fields such as artificial intelligence, biotechnology, and space exploration.

Conclusion:

While investment is a powerful tool for financial progress, it necessitates a combination of knowledge, patience, and strategy. Whether you're a new investor or a seasoned market participant, the key to success is continuous learning and adaptation. Investment can be the wind beneath the wings of financial dreams if one has an eye on the horizon and one's feet firmly set in strong principles.

Chapter 41: Lifestyle Decisions and Their Impact on Financial Independence

Introduction

The path to financial freedom is determined not only by income numbers and investment returns, but also by the numerous lifestyle choices we make. Every decision we make, from what we buy to where we live, has an impact on our financial security. We will look at the significant influences of minimalism, the distinction between desires and necessities, and the strategic approach of geo-arbitrage in this chapter.

Less is More: The Minimalism Movement

Simplicity is an ideology that promotes living with less. It's a shift away from materialism and toward a life filled with experiences, meaning, and purpose.

Impact on Finances: Adopting minimalism frequently results in lower expenses. Individuals who prioritize value and purpose over quantity frequently find themselves saving more, collecting less debt, and enjoying better financial flexibility.

Beyond Materialism: Reduction can provide intangible benefits in addition to real savings. It promotes a contented mood, decreases stress from clutter, and can even lead to enhanced mental well-being, influencing one's financial decisions and outlook indirectly.

A Holistic Approach to Evaluating Wants and Needs

Every purchase can be divided into two categories: wishes and needs. It is critical to distinguish between the two for efficient financial planning.

Defining Needs: These are basic necessities such as food, shelter, and healthcare. Survival and basic well-being would be jeopardized without them.

Defining Wants: These are products or services that provide additional comfort or pleasure but are not required. Luxury things, entertainment, and vacations are some examples.

Financial Implications: Assessing and categorizing spending into desires and needs on a regular basis can lead to improved budgeting. It assists in identifying areas of needless spending, allowing for a more targeted approach to saving and investing.

Geo-arbitrage: Cost-cutting Relocation

Geo-arbitrage entails taking advantage of the disparity in living costs between areas. Individuals can maximize their purchasing power and accelerate their route to financial independence by earning money in a high-income country while living in a low-cost country or region.

Many digital nomads earn wages or revenues comparable to those in the United States or Europe but opt to reside in Southeast Asian countries where the cost of living is substantially lower, maximizing their savings rate.

Considerations: While geo-arbitrage might be lucrative, it is critical to take cultural differences, visa rules, healthcare quality, and personal comfort into mind.

Conclusion

Financial freedom is a product of both thinking and money. Individuals can substantially impact their financial paths by adopting a minimalist attitude, distinguishing between wants and requirements, and carefully choosing where to live. After all, the path to financial independence entails more than just earning more money; it also entails making informed, holistic lifestyle decisions.

Chapter 42: Creating a Personalized Financial Independence Path

At its core, financial independence is not a one-size-fits-all ideology. Individual dreams, values, circumstances, and aspirations shape this highly personal path. This journey does not cease after a specific financial barrier is reached; it evolves and grows, taking on new forms as life unfolds. The beauty is not only in the goal, but also in the journey itself.

Considering Personal Values and Financial Goals

Introspection is the first step in any journey. Before digging into financial techniques or budgeting tools, consider what you genuinely value. Do you want to live a life of travel? Or perhaps you aspire to live in a peaceful rural setting. Perhaps your motivation is philanthropy.

Understanding your personal beliefs serves as a guidepost for your financial decisions. Your values will shape your goals, and your goals will shape the financial techniques you employ.

The Ongoing Process of Learning and Adapting

Global events, technological breakthroughs, and altering economic paradigms all have an impact on the financial environment. Financial independence is thus a dynamic state rather than a static achievement.

Keeping up with financial trends, continuing to educate oneself, and being adaptable are not only useful, but also necessary. Being flexible and knowledgeable guarantees that you're always on the path of growth, whether it's the introduction of a new investment avenue, a change in tax rules, or a worldwide economic shift.

Rejoicing in Past Achievements and Looking Forward to Future Challenges

Every modest step toward financial freedom is a reason for celebration. Did you pay off any outstanding debts? Do you want to buy your first stock? Buying a house? Each of these steppingstones represents your dedication and progress toward financial independence.

However, difficulties are an inevitable part of this path. Economic downturns, personal setbacks, or unanticipated bills can all be obstacles. However, every setback presents an opportunity to learn, adapt, and emerge stronger. Taking on these problems with knowledge and a resilient mindset guarantees that you don't deviate from your route.

Conclusion

The combination of financial knowledge and personal development results in a comprehensive strategy to financial freedom. It's not just about the numbers on a balance sheet; it's also about the life those numbers allow you to live. Remember to enjoy the trip, treasure the lessons learned, and, most importantly, create a story that reflects your own vision of financial freedom.

Module 8:

Legacy of Enlightenment

Empowering Future Generations with Financial Wisdom.

Chapter 43: The Power of Self-Education

In an era where change is the only constant, adaptability and continuous learning are no longer mere attributes; they are necessities. The realm of finance, with its intricacies and dynamic nature, is no exception. Self-education is the beacon that illuminates our financial journey, allowing us to navigate with foresight, precision, and confidence.

The Ever-evolving Landscape of Finance

From the barter systems of ancient civilizations to the cryptocurrency era of today, the financial landscape has been in a state of perpetual evolution. Every decade, if not every year, introduces innovations and shifts, be it in investment instruments, banking systems, or global economic patterns.

Understanding these changes is crucial. The rise of digital currencies, the evolution of stock trading platforms, and even the shifts in global economic powers have direct implications for personal finance decisions. Without an awareness and understanding of these shifts, we risk making decisions based on outdated knowledge, which could lead to missed opportunities or potential pitfalls.

Resources and Platforms for Continuous Learning

Thankfully, the age of the internet has democratized access to knowledge. Here are some resources and platforms to keep you abreast of the latest in finance:

1. **Online Courses:** Websites like Coursera, Udemy, and Khan Academy offer courses on everything from basic personal finance to advanced investment strategies. Many top universities also offer free online courses on economics and finance.

2. **Financial News Platforms:** Websites like Bloomberg, Reuters, and the Financial Times provide up-to-date news on global financial events. Apps like Investopedia offer both news and educational content.

3. **Books:** While the world may be digitizing, books remain an invaluable resource. Authors like Robert Kiyosaki, Dave Ramsey, and Warren Buffet offer timeless advice and insights into the world of money.

4. **Podcasts and Webinars:** The rise of audio content has seen a surge in finance-focused podcasts. These are excellent for those who prefer to learn on-the-go. Webinars also offer interactive ways to learn from experts.

5. **Financial Blogs and Forums:** Websites like the Bogleheads forum or blogs like Mr. Money Mustache offer community-driven insights, advice, and discussions on financial topics.

Case Studies: Success Through Self-Education

1. **Jane's Journey with Cryptocurrency:** Jane, a high school teacher, first read about Bitcoin on an online forum. Intrigued, she embarked on a self-education journey, enrolling in online courses, participating in webinars, and joining cryptocurrency communities. Her informed investments in various digital currencies not only augmented her income but also secured her retirement.

2. **Alex's Adventures in Stock Trading:** With no formal education in finance, Alex's introduction to stocks came through a podcast. This spurred him to delve deeper, using

platforms like Investopedia and financial news apps to educate himself. Today, Alex manages a successful portfolio, all thanks to his commitment to continuous learning.

3. **Sam's Sustainable Investments:** Inspired by a book on sustainable living, Sam decided to invest solely in eco-friendly businesses. Through blogs, online courses, and financial news platforms, he identified green companies with promising returns. His investments not only yield profit but also contribute to a greener planet.

In conclusion, the vast sea of finance might appear daunting, but with the power of self- education, anyone can navigate it successfully. The resources are at our fingertips; all it takes is the will to learn, the curiosity to explore, and the wisdom to apply this knowledge in our financial endeavors. Remember, in the realm of finance, the most potent investment is the one made in oneself.

Chapter 44: Inculcating a Growth Mindset

At the crossroads of psychology and financial planning, lies an essential and often overlooked ingredient for wealth creation: a growth mindset. Unlike a fixed mindset, which views abilities as static, a growth mindset thrives on challenges, sees effort as a path to mastery, and perceives failures as opportunities for growth. Within the realm of finance, this perspective plays a pivotal role in determining how individuals navigate their financial journey.

The Psychological Aspects of Wealth Creation

The creation of wealth is not just a mathematical exercise; it's a deeply psychological process. Our financial behaviors, often, are a reflection of our beliefs, attitudes, and values. Some key psychological aspects include:

1. **Belief Systems:** What we were taught about money during our formative years significantly shapes our financial behaviors. For instance, if money was a taboo topic in a household, it might lead to financial anxiety in adulthood.

2. **Risk Tolerance:** This is inherently psychological. While some individuals are adventurous, embracing high-risk, high-reward ventures, others might be more conservative, opting for stability even if it means lower returns.

3. **Reward Mechanisms:** The brain's dopamine-driven reward system can influence financial decisions. Instant gratifications, like impulsive purchases, can spike dopamine levels, whereas

long-term investments, though more rewarding, may not offer immediate dopamine boosts.

Embracing Failures and Setbacks as Learning Opportunities

Every investor, no matter how seasoned, has faced setbacks. Stock market crashes, failed ventures, or unforeseen expenditures - these are an inevitable part of the financial journey. However, the difference lies in perception.

1. Analyzing Failures: Instead of viewing financial setbacks as defeats, see them as lessons. What went wrong? Were there any red flags missed? Analyzing failures can provide insights that safeguard future investments.

2. Resilience: Financial setbacks can be demotivating. However, with a growth mindset, resilience becomes a cornerstone. It's not about the number of times one falls but the ability to bounce back with even more determination.

3. Continuous Learning: Embracing failures means being open to learning. Whether it's revisiting investment strategies or seeking mentorship after a failed venture, every setback can pave the way for future successes.

Harnessing Positivity and Vision for Financial Success

A clear vision, coupled with a positive outlook, can act as the North Star for financial endeavors.

1. **Visualizing Success:** Visual imagery is powerful. By visualizing financial goals, be it buying a dream house or achieving a specific net worth, individuals can keep their motivation levels high and stay on course.

2. **Positive Affirmations:** While it might sound clichéd, positive affirmations can reshape thought patterns, transforming financial anxieties into proactive financial planning.

3. **Setting Clear Milestones:** Instead of vague goals like "I want to be wealthy," setting clear milestones like "I aim to save $20,000 by the end of the year" can offer direction and purpose.

In conclusion, while numbers, strategies, and financial instruments are critical, the real game- changer lies in mindset. A growth mindset, characterized by adaptability, resilience, and an insatiable hunger for learning, can turn financial dreams into tangible realities. When paired with actionable strategies, this mindset can be the compass guiding individuals through the tumultuous seas of finance, ensuring they reach the shores of their envisioned financial success.

Chapter 45: Empowering the Next Generation: Financial Education for Children

Teaching kids about money is like teaching them to ride a bike. Start with training wheels, give them a gentle push, and before you know it, they're cruising on their own. Financial education can give kids the skills they need to make smart money choices as they grow.

Introducing Money Concepts at Different Ages

Just as you wouldn't hand a toddler a bicycle and expect them to ride, it's essential to introduce money ideas that match a child's age.

- **Toddlers and Preschoolers:** Start with the basics. Let them recognize coins and bills. A simple piggy bank can be a fun way for them to save a few pennies.

- **Elementary School Kids:** Now's the time to chat about the value of money. They can learn that things cost money and start understanding the difference between wants and needs.

- **Middle Schoolers:** Introduce the concept of earning. Maybe they can earn money through chores or a small allowance. Discuss how to save, spend, and share their earnings.

- **High School Kids:** Dive deeper into topics like budgeting, saving for big goals, and even the basics of investing.

Games, Books, and Tools to Teach Financial Literacy to Kids

Learning about money should be fun! Here are some ways to make it entertaining:

- **Games:** Board games like "Monopoly" or card games like "Pay Day" are not just fun; they also introduce kids to money management and decision-making.

- **Books:** There are many kids' books that talk about money. "Lemonade in Winter" or "The Berenstain Bears' Trouble with Money" are good picks.

- **Apps and Online Tools:** In today's digital age, there are loads of apps and websites designed to teach kids about money.

Cultivating a Saving and Investment Habit Early On

Starting good money habits young can set kids up for a financially smart future.

- **Open a Savings Account:** Take them to a bank and open a savings account in their name. This can be an exciting way for them to see their money grow.

- **Match Their Savings:** To encourage saving, consider matching what they save. If they save $5, you can add in another $5. It's like their very own company match!

- **Introduce Simple Investment Ideas:** As they get older, talk about how money can "work" for them. Maybe buy them a share in a company they like and track the stock together.

- In the end, teaching kids about money is about setting them up for success. It's giving them the tools they need to make informed decisions. So, when the time comes, they're ready to pedal fast, make a few turns, and handle any bumps in the road with confidence.

Chapter 46: Creating a Financial Legacy

Leaving behind a legacy is like planting a tree. You might not always be there to enjoy its shade, but future generations can benefit from it. It's about ensuring that what you've built and learned doesn't end with you but continues to provide for and guide those who come after.

The Importance of Estate Planning and Wills

Imagine you've built a lovely sandcastle. Wouldn't you want to protect it from the waves? That's what estate planning and wills do for your hard-earned assets.

- **Estate Planning:** This is just a fancy term for deciding how your things (like money, property, or other assets) will be shared when you're not around. It helps ensure that your wishes are followed.

- **Wills:** A will is like a letter you leave behind, telling everyone what you'd like done with your stuff. It's a way to make sure your favorite necklace goes to your niece, or your prized book collection ends up with someone who'll cherish it.

Ethical Investments and Philanthropy: Leaving a Mark on the World

Remember how good it feels to help someone out or do something for the planet? That feeling can continue, even when you're not around.

- **Ethical Investments:** These are choices you make to put your money in places that match your values. Maybe you invest in companies that take care of the environment or stand for social causes you believe in.

- **Philanthropy:** This is a big word that simply means giving to causes or people in need. It could be donating to a local school, supporting a charity, or funding a community project. It's your way of leaving a lasting, positive mark on the world.

The Art of Passing Down Stories, Values, and Financial Principles

Money isn't the only thing you leave behind. Your stories, lessons, and values can be even more precious.

- **Stories:** Remember the tales your grandparents told you? Those stories carried lessons, history, and a sense of belonging. Share your stories, the ups and downs, the joys and struggles, so they can be a guide or comfort for those who come after.

- **Values:** The beliefs and principles that guided your life can be your most significant legacy. Whether it's the value of hard work, the importance of kindness, or the belief in always learning, passing these on can shape future generations.

- **Financial Principles:** Just like a favorite recipe, the financial lessons you've learned can be passed down. Maybe it's the importance of saving, the thrill of smart investing, or the satisfaction of living within one's means. Sharing these can equip your loved ones for their own financial journeys.

In the grand tapestry of life, we're all threads, weaving our own stories. Creating a financial legacy ensures that our thread, our color, and our pattern continue to be part of the design, enriching it for years and generations to come.

Appendix: Navigating Further Exploration

Recommended Books, Courses, and Seminars

This section serves as a compass for your continued exploration of financial wisdom and AI innovation. Discover a curated selection of books, online courses, and seminars that delve deeper into the intersection of ancient insights and modern technology. Immerse yourself in these resources to gain a more profound understanding of enlightened financial growth.

Financial Tools and Apps for Different Age Groups

Unlock a world of practical financial tools and apps tailored to various life stages. Whether you're just starting out, in the prime of your career, or preparing for retirement, this collection of resources empowers you to manage your finances effectively. Explore budgeting apps, investment platforms, retirement calculators, and more that align with your specific financial needs.

Organizations and Foundations Promoting Financial Literacy

Connect with a network of organizations and foundations that are committed to promoting financial literacy and empowerment. Discover resources that offer guidance, workshops, and educational materials designed to equip individuals with the knowledge and skills to navigate the financial landscape with confidence. Engage with these initiatives to amplify your financial acumen and contribute to a financially literate society.

To fully leverage the potential of this appendix:

- **Curate:** Select resources that resonate with your interests and financial goals, tailoring your exploration to your unique journey.

- **Explore:** Delve into the recommended books, courses, and tools, allowing each resource to expand your understanding of enlightened finance.

- **Engage:** Connect with organizations and foundations promoting financial literacy, participating in their programs and initiatives to deepen your knowledge.

- **Apply:** Incorporate financial tools and apps into your daily life, using them as instruments to enhance your financial decision-making.

- **Share:** Share your discoveries and experiences with friends, family, or online communities, contributing to a culture of informed financial exploration.

As you navigate this appendix, you're equipped with a roadmap for further exploration and empowerment. The resources offered here enable you to embark on a continuous journey of learning, growth, and connection, as you merge the wisdom of the past with the possibilities of the future.

Final thoughts

It's ironic that in a society humming with technological developments, age-old wisdom stays evergreen, leading us through life's complicated tapestry. The secret of financial wealth is found at the crossroads of old knowledge and modern innovation. While artificial intelligence and technology bring tools and resources, it is the timeless values that provide direction and purpose. This handbook aims to investigate this synergy, providing a comprehensive path to financial freedom.

Ancient Wisdom from the Sands of Time

Civilizations have prospered throughout history on fundamental characteristics such as patience, discipline, integrity, and foresight. These are the pillars upon which any lasting wealth is constructed.

Patience: Just as a farmer must wait for the seasons to change before reaping the advantages of a crop planted months ago, wealth growth requires patience. It highlights the concept of delayed gratification, emphasizing that actual wealth is built up through time.

Discipline: The key is consistency. Ancient rites and practices stressed consistency, and the same holds true for financial habits. The foundation of financial growth is regular savings, persistent investments, and habitual learning.

Integrity requires not only honesty and transparency with others, but also with oneself. Understanding one's financial situation, admitting debts, and setting realistic goals are all part of this process.

Foresight: Whether in agriculture, warfare, or diplomacy, ancient civilizations prospered on their ability to anticipate obstacles. Foresight in finance refers to planning, budgeting, and forecasting future demands and market trends.

The AI Revolution: Cutting-Edge Technology at Your Fingertips Artificial intelligence and technology have democratized access to global information, providing tools that supplement traditional wisdom.

Personalized Financial Assistants: AI-powered platforms may evaluate spending patterns, provide budgeting guidance, and even forecast future financial requirements.

Global Investment Platforms: Technology has blurred borders. You may now invest in equities all across the world, participate in peer-to-peer lending, and research international real estate markets with the press of a mouse.

Continuous Learning: AI-curated learning modules may keep you up to date on the newest financial trends, keeping you one step ahead of the competition.

Automated Risk Assessment: Using complicated algorithms, AI systems can provide insights into the potential hazards connected with particular investments, assisting in informed decision- making.

Practical Advice for the Next Generation

Respect the Process: Just as a seed does not become a tree overnight, wealth does not accumulate overnight. Accept the path, knowing that it requires persistent effort, wise judgments, and time.

Leverage Global Knowledge: With the internet, you have access to all of the world's knowledge at your fingertips. Participate in online courses, keep up with global financial trends, and communicate with international financial communities.

Balance Technology and Wisdom: While AI provides tools, old principles should guide your decisions. Rather than replacing age-old wisdom, use technology to apply it.

Avoid the 'Get Rich Quick' Illusion: Be wary of schemes and projects that promise quick riches. Most of the time, these are delusions that can result in considerable losses.

Conclusion

True financial freedom exists at the intersection of time-tested knowledge and cutting-edge innovation. By combining ancient teachings with modern instruments, one can create a financially prosperous and enlightened future. Remember that the route to wealth is about the insights, experiences, and growth along the way, not simply the goal

Glossary

- **Abundance:** The state of having plentiful wealth; the opposite of scarcity.

- **AI (Artificial Intelligence):** Computer systems able to perform tasks that normally require human intelligence, such as visual perception, speech recognition, decision-making, and translation between languages.

- **Asset Allocation:** The implementation of an investment strategy that seeks to balance risk versus reward by adjusting the percentage of each asset in an investment portfolio.

- **Barter System:** An ancient system where goods and services were exchanged for other goods and services without using money.

- **Blockchain:** A digital ledger in which transactions are recorded chronologically and publicly.

- **Budgeting:** The process of creating a plan to spend your money.

- **Cause and Effect:** The principle of causation; understanding that every action has a consequence.

- **Currency Evolution:** The transformation of money over time, from tangible items like coins to digital currencies like cryptocurrency.

- **Emotional Intelligence:** The ability to identify and manage one's own emotions, as well as the emotions of others.

- **Estate Planning:** The act of preparing for the transfer of a person's wealth and assets after his or her death.

- **Ethical Investing:** The practice of investing in companies that are considered socially conscious in their business dealings or directly promote environmental responsibility.

- **Financial Independence:** A state where one has enough wealth to no longer need to work to live.

- **Financial Legacy:** Money and other assets left to a person or institution, such as a charity, after death.

- **Geo-arbitrage:** The act of taking advantage of the price differences between two or more markets.

- **Legacy:** Something handed down from an ancestor or a predecessor or from the past.

- **Mindfulness:** A mental state achieved by focusing one's awareness on the present moment.

- **Philanthropy**: The desire to help others, particularly through the donation of money to good causes.

- **Retirement**: The action or fact of leaving one's job and ceasing to work.

- **Risk Management**: Identifying, assessing, and prioritizing risks followed by coordinated and economical application of resources to minimize, monitor, and control the probability or impact of unfortunate events.

- **Self-Education**: Learning or teaching oneself outside of a formal educational institution.

- **Universal Law of Attraction**: A popular belief that positive or negative thoughts bring positive or negative experiences into a person's life.

- **Wealth Accumulation**: The process of acquiring an increasing number or quantity of valuable assets and financial resources.

Congratulations, Thank You, and Next Steps

Dear Reader,

First and foremost, congrats on finishing this journey between ancient knowledge and the cutting-edge landscapes of artificial intelligence in finance. Your journey from the start to the last page demonstrates your commitment to a brighter, more enlightened financial future.

Thank you for selecting this guide as your travel companion. Your trust and time are priceless, and I'm honored to have been a part of this chapter in your life.

Put Your Learning into Action: Begin by implementing the tactics and insights that spoke to you the most. Remember that the path to financial freedom is distinguished by little, steady actions.

Share and Grow Together: Share your knowledge with friends, family, and online groups. This not only reinforces your comprehension, but it can also motivate others on their financial journey.

Feedback Influences the Future: If a specific chapter touched you or you believe there is need for improvement, please let me know. Your feedback could help others who are navigating these seas.

Your reading adventure is over, but your path to financial enlightenment and empowerment is only getting started. Here's to a prosperous future filled with growth, wisdom, and wisdom.

With warmth and gratitude, Anant

217